SOCCER FOR JUNIORS

By the same author:

The Persuader
Loophole or How to Rob a Bank

SOCCER FOR JUNIORS

by

Robert Pollock

Charles Scribner's Sons   ○   New York

First Charles Scribner's Sons Paperback Edition 1983

Cover pictures: Robert Pollock
Training pictures: Robert Pollock

Library of Congress Cataloging in Publication Data

Pollock, Robert.
  Soccer for juniors.
  Includes index.
  1. Soccer for children.   I. Title.
GV944.2.P64   796.334   79-29704
ISBN 0-684-17974-1

    3 5 7 9 11 13 15 17 19   F/P   20 18 16 14 12 10 8 6 4 2

Printed in the United States of America

For Ben—a good left-winger

and

the soccer youth of America

Acknowledgments

The author wishes to sincerely acknowledge the very valuable contributions made by the following people and organizations in the preparation of this book:

Joseph R. Bartis, D.P.M.
Oakland, California

James P. Nevins, M.D.
Berkeley, California

Donald Greer
Chairman, United States Youth
    Soccer Association

Lynn Berling
Associate Publisher and
    Editor-in-Chief, *Soccer America*

Hans de Graef, Coach of the
    Walnut Creek Sharks, and the
    members of that team

Amelie Austin

Adidas Shoe Inc., and Mitre Sports

The author would also like to thank the young soccer players shown on the cover and in the instruction photographs for their generous cooperation: Ben Pollock and Greg Sosa, both of whom played for the 1979 undefeated U-14 California State Select team, and Michael Gaither of the Walnut Creek Superscoops.

Contents

CONTENTS

SOCCER FOR JUNIORS

INTRODUCTION

In whatever way you become involved in soccer, there is immense pleasure to be had from the sport. It is a marvelous way of learning the rules and conduct of life, for, after all, we are all on a team of some kind or another.

Although in this book all soccer players are referred to as "he," it must be emphasized that soccer is a game for both sexes, and that one out of every four young people who play in America is a girl—quite a large number, compared to other sports.

A Background to American Soccer

The actual origins of soccer are complicated, because the game was invented several times in different places. For example, the Chinese had a version called *Tsu-chu*. In Mexico, Indians continue to play up and down the rocky hills. The ancient Greeks had a kicking game, and so did the Romans, who reportedly got started when two bored soldiers began kicking around a stone (some say it was a head).

The game grew, and during the Middle Ages, towns would compete with hundreds of players on each side trying to score in goals that might be located miles apart. Predictably, this form was violent and often banned. When the private schools in England adopted the game in the early nineteenth century, rules that emphasized fair play were introduced, and the game became known as association football. (It is still called football, in fact, in every country except the United States.)

At one of these private schools, Rugby, a young man named William Webb Ellis decided, for unrecorded reasons, to pick up the ball and run with it—something not done in football at the time. This unprecedented action eventually led to a different game, called rugby in memory of its birthplace.

Across the Atlantic, Americans started by playing football in the soccer style, such as in the Rutgers–Princeton game of 1869. But Harvard, which had played rugby at McGill University in Canada, introduced the egg-shaped ball of that game, changed a few rules to accommodate the other colleges, and helped establish football as we know it today. As a result, soccer declined as an intercollegiate sport, and was played mainly in the cities of the East, which were heavily populated by European immigrants.

But following the end of World War II, soccer once again gained in popularity, because of the influx of immigrants from a then-battered Europe. The one exception to the usual foreign teams playing in U.S. cities was St. Louis, which had a superbly organized youth and adult program that produced teams largely made up of Americans.

It was St. Louis that provided the bulk of the players, mostly part-time professionals playing for small, unknown clubs for the United States team, that went to the 1950 World

Cup competition in Brazil. The Americans shocked the soccer-football fraternity by beating the favorite, England, 1–0.

The English were so confident of winning that they had kept Stanley Matthews, the greatest dribbler ever, off their roster to avoid an injury. They were saving him for a game that never materialized.

The United States surprised the soccer world again in 1966 by announcing that an assorted group of millionaires had decided to invest in U.S. soccer franchises. What followed was the formation of various rival groups, all vying for recognition and profit. The venture ended in financial failure.

It was not until 1973 that soccer in the United States began its climb toward a more widespread acceptance. The various new groups formed themselves into one major group, the North American Soccer League, creating, with the American Soccer League, the nucleus of a growing professional organization. Attendance was up, and the news media at last recognized that youth interest in soccer was beginning to sweep the country.

But in the years to come, the official history of U.S. soccer will probably identify 1975 as the year in which the game truly emerged as a national sport. In the summer of that year President Gerald R. Ford invited to the White House a man who was renowned as the greatest sportsman in the world: Pelé.

The president said, "I'm sure your presence will increase American interest in soccer. We have a lot of young people who are now learning to play. Eventually we may even be able to compete in world championships."

The great Pelé had signed to play for a North American Soccer League team called the New York Cosmos.

Soccer in America exploded.

The Game

Soccer is a game played by two opposing teams, each having a maximum of eleven players on the field.

The team that wins is the one that scores the most goals—a goal being when the whole of the ball passes over the goal line and between the upright goalposts.

One of the eleven players is the goalkeeper. He is the only one allowed to place his hands on the ball, and he can only do this in the penalty area. If he comes out of that area, then the rules applying to the rest of the team come into force; that is, if he touches the ball with his hands, he commits an infringement.

When the ball goes out of play, either by passing over the goal line or one of the touchlines (or sidelines), it is brought back into play by a member of the team who did not put it out of play. This means if the ball goes out over a touchline, a throw-in is awarded; if it goes out over the goal line, a goal kick is awarded; and if the defense put the ball out over the goal line, a corner kick is awarded to the attacking team.

The field is divided into two halves, and the choice of which team plays on which half is decided by the toss of a coin. The two captains join the referee, who tosses the coin. The captain who wins the toss can elect either to kick off or to defend a particular half.

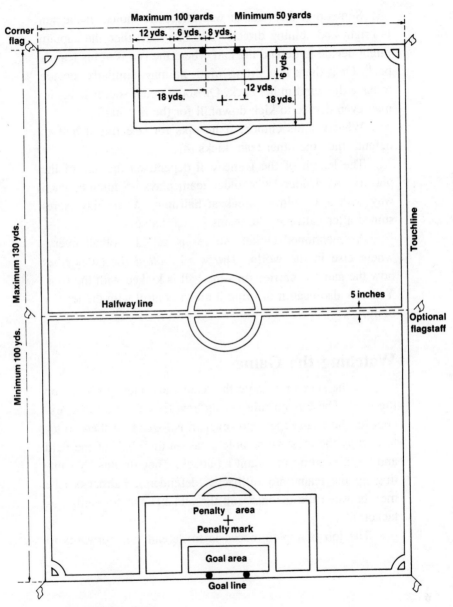

1. The playing field.

Sometimes the weather will affect the choice. If the sun is bright and shining directly into one half, then the captain might decide to defend the half where the sun is at his team's back. Or if there is a strong wind, he may, similarly, decide to have the wind in his back. On some youth-soccer fields he may even decide to kick downhill for the first half.

Whatever his choice, if he opts for selecting a half to defend, then the other team kicks off.

The length of the game will depend on the age of the players. An Under-19 or older team plays 45 minutes each way with a 10-minute break at halftime. When play is resumed after halftime, the teams switch halves.

As mentioned earlier, soccer is called football everywhere else in the world. The word *football* best describes how the game is carried on—the ball is kicked with the foot. You can also head it or bring it under control with the legs or body.

Watching the Game

At the start of a game the teams take their positions on the field. There is no rule saying how they must do this, except for the goalkeeper. However, it is logical for them to try to occupy the most vulnerable areas on their half of the field and be in position to mount an attack. They do this by splitting up the team into fullbacks (defenders), halfbacks (the men between the defense and the attack), and forwards (attackers).

The job of the fullbacks is to defend, the forwards to

attack, and the halfbacks to act as a link between the two.

It is from this principle that much argument and discussion have evolved, the outcome of which has been formations—the way in which the players position themselves and what part of the field becomes their individual responsibility. (Formations are discussed in detail in another chapter.)

The most common formation in all age groups, whether amateur or professional, is called a 4–3–3. This indicates four fullbacks, three halfbacks, and three forwards.

The whistle blows and play begins. What follows will depend on the ability of the players. It can be anything from a puffing, grunting group of older chaps to fleet-footed youngsters to superstar professionals. It can also be a tough rushing game, a well-paced controlled exhibition of skill, or even a combination of all elements.

Not all soccer players are physically large. In fact, some of them may be relatively small. The great dribbler Stanley Matthews was a short, lightly built, bowlegged man. He could make a 6-foot fullback look very foolish as he bedazzled him with his superb ball control and body swerves time after time. Pelé is well under 6 feet.

Generally, most youth teams have one or two players who are more obviously talented than others. They are easy to spot because they are given the ball more often by their own, less talented teammates. But here again, the better the team, the less obvious the stars. The reason for this is that the game will be distributed better; it will cover the whole field of play and not just the area in which the stars operate.

As you become more familiar with the game, you will

begin to appreciate the less flashy player, having gained understanding of his ability and function. He might be a fullback—fullbacks do not do too much dribbling and so are less obvious—but you will see how well he covers his part of the defense and how he marks an attacker and leaves him with little space in which to maneuver.

Or he might be a halfback. You can almost see a good halfback think. One way to pick this up is to watch the halfback line when they do not have the ball. If they are any good at all, they will not be standing around waiting for the action. They will be watching the play, setting up for what may become an attack, or be back in the defensive part of the field ready to support the fullbacks.

You will hear a lot about the use and creation of space on the field. Some people find this difficult to understand, and so do many players. Basically, it means that a player who traditionally operates in a particular part of the field makes room by varying his position.

For instance, the left wing will move up and down a corridor parallel to the left sideline. (As the team becomes more advanced, this will not always hold true.) The defending right back will normally try to mark him. It is the winger's job to move around in his area so that the marking becomes difficult.

If the winger moves toward the center of the field, the fullback will move with him, thus leaving open the area, or space, occupied previously by the winger and the fullback. The winger has thus created open space that can be put to good use by, say, the left half.

Allied with the use of space is pace. Some teams try to

go full pelt for the length of the game, and you will see a tremendous amount of rushing around—a continuous all-out effort. This seldom works well, although it often looks as if the team is commanding the game.

The teams that tend to control the games are those who vary the pace. The halfbacks work a series of short passes until they see a hole in the defense; then they strike.

While it is important for forwards to have speed, the style of speed that works best is speed to the ball. You will often hear spectators calling out from the sidelines, "They're beating you to the ball." This means just that: that the other team is faster off the mark and gets possession of the ball first.

This is why soccer calls for quick reactions. A player must be capable of instant movement; otherwise, he will end up continually chasing players who have gained possession of the ball before him.

So it can be seen that a good soccer game is not just two teams playing kickball with each other. There has to be method, control, and finesse. This takes time not only for the players to accomplish, but for spectators to appreciate.

Soccer as a Career

It is the dream of every talented young athlete to perform in his own personal superdome stadium. To the soccer player, this means the final game in the World Cup.

More than one hundred thousand people sit in the stadium, suddenly hushed and tense; millions more are in front of television sets around the world. There can only be minutes before the referee blows the final whistle. The score is 2–2. The players are weary, but they strain to pull out their last ounce of strength to make that one final effort.

The ball comes free. It is picked up by number 11 in open space. He's away, he's away; it's an incredible run; he cuts in to narrow the angle; he shoots. It's a goal, it's a goal; the United States has won the World Cup. For the first time in the history of soccer, the United States has won the World Cup.

The crowd explodes. Players rush to number 11. They grab him, hug him, and raise him high on their shoulders as they march around the field, triumphant. The crowd is on its feet, cheering and waving its new hero.

A young boy comes out of his reverie, straightens his soccer socks, and runs out onto a wet field. Maybe today he might get a goal, he thinks. It's about time.

It could happen, and it is not only the dream of young boys but of a growing number of adults—that one day the United States might win the World Cup. Not the next one, but the one after that, perhaps.

It is ironic that the man who was considered to be the greatest soccer player in the world, Pelé, played his final games in one of the last countries in the world to adopt his sport.

On the face of it, this very fact makes the United States a good place for a young soccer star to emerge; there is less competition.

There are, of course, two sides to that coin. Fierce competition breeds greater ambition and effort and, in turn, more dedicated players. A major criticism of American soccer players is that they do not have this fierce dedication. As one very well-known coach put it, "American kids don't start playing until ten minutes into the game."

That the talent has not yet bloomed in the United States to any great extent provides a platform for the argument put forth by the professional and collegiate coaches when they hand out places on their rosters to foreign players. The unfortunate fact is that the most successful "American" soccer teams are predominantly a collection of players from other countries playing under the U.S. flag.

There are a number of routes a young man can take in an effort to become a professional soccer player. One is through a local association of the USYSA, the United States Youth Soccer Association, which is the governing body in most states. It is affiliated with the USSF, the United States Soccer Federation, and thence with FIFA, the Fédération Internationale de Football Association, the governing body worldwide.

There are other youth-soccer associations in the country, although few of them have the same organizational scope as the USYSA. They also lack the direct affiliation with FIFA.

The young player who has a professional career in mind might begin by trying to play on a local team that could possibly win its way to a state cup, or perhaps by being chosen to play for a "select" (all-star) team in his division. Either way he can hope to be noticed and selected to play for his state's team.

If the player is good enough, he might eventually play for the Junior National team, which provides an entry to Olympic selection. The benefits are marvelous—a summer of soccer at training camps around the country and even travel abroad to gain international playing experience.

Somewhere along the line, the exceptional young player may be spotted by a member of the coaching staff from a university and, if he is really lucky, be offered either a full or partial scholarship. Or he could be picked up by a professional scout and become part of the system whereby, although he signs to play for the pro team, the team contributes to the cost of a college education. Under this system the player retains his amateur status, thus keeping open the option for Olympic selection.

If the player manages the college route, and if he maintains and develops his talent, he can become part of the college/pro soccer draft. A player does not, however, have to go to college to be drafted. The North American Soccer League (NASL), has added a rule that calls for all NASL teams to form reserve teams beginning in 1980.

This rule has created the need for more players with professional potential, and the pro teams are now drafting directly from the high schools.

There are twenty-four teams—franchises actually—in the NASL, and they may carry a roster of seventeen or more players. A young player signed from either the college or high-school drafts can expect to earn, on the average, $12,000 to $18,000 a year.

Naturally, if a player develops international superstar status, then the sky's the limit.

The NASL is not the only professional soccer organization in the United States. The American Soccer League (ASL), which was originally centered in the East Coast cities, has now spread throughout the country and has twelve teams.

Considered to be the lesser of the two leagues, and in fact rather looked down upon by the NASL, the ASL is more concerned with the development of American players. They also draft from the colleges and high schools.

Here again, a young player can expect to earn about $1,000 a month, and he may be offered either a twelve-month contract or a seasonal one of five months.

There is always talk about the possibility of the two leagues merging. Most of the discussions have been less than unofficial, and the whole subject is hampered by the attitudes of the leagues toward one another. The ASL, being the elder of the two, considers itself more than equal to the brash newcomer. It has been suggested that the leagues should hold a soccer equivalent to the football Super Bowl. The way the teams are placed at the moment in their respective leagues, a soccer super bowl could pit the New York Cosmos from the NASL against the New York Apollos of the ASL.

This is basically the structure of professional soccer in the United States. It is developing and expanding very, very swiftly—some people would say scrambling—in an effort to accomplish two objectives: to make money and to be taken seriously by the rest of the soccer world.

One problem facing some young players who want to use soccer as a way of helping themselves through college or who want to become professionals is being certain that their talent is recognized. Because of the widely varying abilities of the many hundreds of youth teams in the United States, a very good player can quite easily get lost in the shuffle because the local team on which he plays never gets anywhere.

It doesn't win a league, never gets anywhere in the state cup or even in any of the divisional tournaments. So who is going to be watching and scouting? The answer is to contact the nearest college or professional team by letter, asking if they are going to hold tryouts or if they would be prepared to send a scout out to look at a player.

Most soccer organizations will agree to help, particularly if the parent's or youth's letter is accompanied by a recommendation from his coach. In fact, there is a growing number of professional teams organizing youth tryouts as part of their community involvement and promotion.

If there is any doubt about whom to contact, the following headquarters of the various soccer groups would be pleased to send full details:

USSF National Headquarters
350 Fifth Avenue
Suite 4010
New York, N.Y. 10001
(Also write to this address for your local State Association, addressed to the Youth Coordinator, USYSA.)

United States Olympic Committee
Olympic House
57 Park Avenue
New York, N.Y. 10016

NCAA
P.O. Box 1906
Shawnee Mission, Kans. 66222

NASL
1133 Avenue of the Americas
New York, N.Y. 10036

ASL
770 Lexington Avenue
New York, N.Y. 10021

Of course, before the dream of playing in the World Cup can come anywhere near reality, a young player has to learn not only how to play the game but how to live it.

The sooner he starts, the better his chances of attaining that dream.

BASIC SKILLS

A Beginning

Every year around August, as the NASL professional season winds down, youngsters start thinking about the forthcoming youth program. More and more of them are deciding to take to the fields.

Youth soccer is divided into definite age groups, the birthday cutoff point being January 1 of the seasonal year, the season usually being from September through March.

The Under-8 group are players who have not reached their eighth birthday before January 1 of the seasonal year. (In other words, if the boy is eight on December 31, he must play in the Under-10 division. But if his birthday falls just one day later, January 1, he plays in the Under-8 group.) The remaining age groups—Under 10, Under 12, Under 14, Under 16, and Under 19—have the same ruling.

The age makeup of a team can become very important. For instance, if half a team's players have their birthdays near the end of the year and the other half have theirs near the beginning, they will have to split up as they move up through the age divisions. Part of the team will have to play in the next age group, the remainder staying put.

Some coaches have been known to reject players because of this factor, the idea being that a team made up of players of similar birthdates can go all the way from Under 8 to Under 19 as a unit.

The length of the game and the size and weight of the ball used also vary within the age groups. The following rules have been established by the USYSA and are used throughout the country:

Division	Game Length	Ball Size	Circumference and Weight
Under 8	2–20 min. halves	No. 4	25″–26″ 11–13 oz.
Under 10	2–25 min. halves	No. 4	25″–26″ 11–13 oz.
Under 12	2–30 min. halves	No. 4	25″–26″ 11–13 oz.
Under 14	2–35 min. halves	No. 5	27″–28″ 14–16 oz.
Under 16	2–40 min. halves	No. 5	27″–28″ 14–16 oz.
Under 19	2–45 min. halves	No. 5	27″–28″ 14–16 oz.

Although a No. 4 ball is indicated for the Under-8 group, the specifications are actually for a No. 3, which is 23 to 24 inches in circumference and 8 to 10 ounces in weight. However, the No. 3 ball is so difficult to obtain in many parts of the United States that the larger size is acceptable. Under-8 players seem to manage the bigger ball quite well.

The Tryouts

Tryouts are organized by the volunteer members of the local youth-soccer clubs. The youngsters are separated into age groups and given a series of athletic tests to perform. For example, they will be asked to run 50 or 100 yards, with the times being recorded, and to dribble a ball between a series of cones, set about a yard apart, again being timed and evaluated.

The tryouts are not a competitive event. What is looked for at tryouts is physical coordination, enthusiasm, attitude, and willingness. Intelligence helps, too, although there is something called soccer intelligence which has nothing at all to do with grade levels.

The scrimmage is probably the most important test at tryouts. It is at this point that the selectors can determine which youngsters might have some ability. Does he just kick at the ball indiscriminately, or does he seem to have some idea of the direction it's supposed to go? But even an experienced coach, who has judged and trained young soccer players for years, will have a difficult job trying to predict, at a single viewing, how the individuals in an Under-10 group are going to turn out. The one exception might be the goalkeeper, since goalkeepers are the only players allowed to handle the ball. They are also the only players who have a fixed area of ground in which to operate.

Formations and Positions

The first tactical decision to be made in forming a new team is the system of play to be used. There has been endless debate about the psychology and tactics of formations. A major principle is that the collective skills of the players available should be the deciding factor.

A predetermined formation should never be master; quite the opposite, the players are masters of the formation.

If a team is heavy on fullbacks, then it should have a formation which makes the most use of them while developing the forward line.

Years ago almost every team played the established formation of 2–3–5. (You should always count the formation from the backs forward, and not, as many people seem to do, from the forwards backward. Soccer numbering starts with the goalkeeper, who is number 1, and ends with the left winger, number 11.) A 2–3–5 formation is two fullbacks, three halfbacks, and five forwards—obviously an attacking setup.

Later there developed a very successful defensive system, 4–2–4. The problem about this, though, particularly for young players, is that it tends to overload the two halfbacks. A further variation is the 4–4–2, but again, as far as young players are concerned, this doesn't give much opportunity to develop an attack because it leaves two men, in this instance forwards, with too much responsibility.

Basically, there are two other systems of play to choose from, and in most cases they are the ones best suited to a young team. The first, and most popular, is 3–3–4. There are three fullbacks, three halfbacks, and four forwards. This is an attacking formation and is generally very successful. It is also an easy formation to teach and one that most new players fall into very quickly.

A system that is growing in popularity is the one first used by a quiet, unassuming soccer genius called Sir Alf Ramsay, manager of the England World Cup team in 1966.

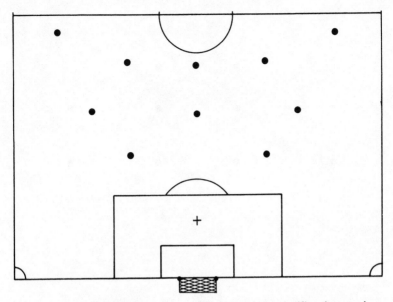

2. The 2–3–5 formation. Two fullbacks, three halfbacks, and five forwards.

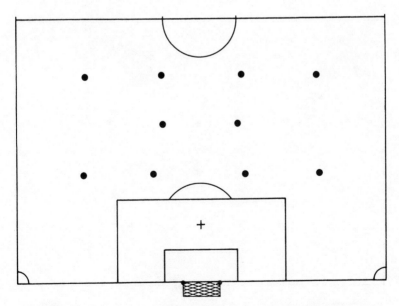

3. The 4–2–4 formation. Four fullbacks, two halfbacks, and four forwards.

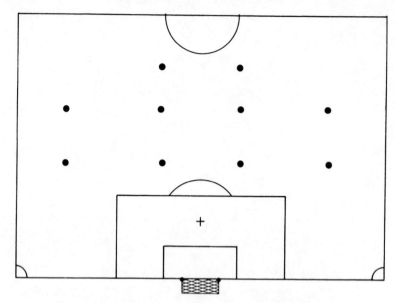

4. The 4–4–2 formation. Four fullbacks, four halfbacks, and two forwards.

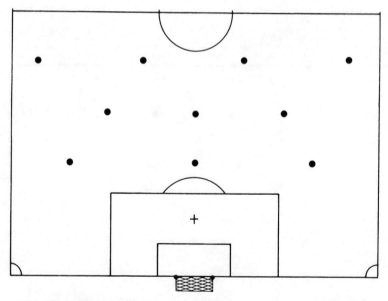

5. The 3–3–4 formation. Three fullbacks, three halfbacks, and four forwards.

His idea was at the time revolutionary, but it eventually influenced the whole of soccer and won England its first World Cup.

The system is 4–3–3. There are four fullbacks plus a three-man halfback line and a three-man forward line. The crux of this formation is to have a strong halfback line—the powerhouse of the team. They must have both speed and stamina.

The arrows on the 4–3–3 diagram show how the formation can alter when it goes into attack. The forward wingmen—outside left and right—move out to the wings, and the two outside halfbacks come up to inside forward

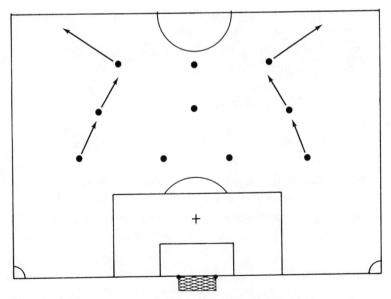

6. The 4–3–3 formation. Four fullbacks, three halfbacks, and three forwards. On attack this formation can become 2-3-5.

positions. Their place is taken by the two outside backs. This produces the old W formation of 2–3–5. In defense, the team quickly reverts to its original 4–3–3 system, and from this it can be seen how important the halfbacks are.

The key to making this formation work is flow and a complete understanding by all the players of the uses of position and space.

A study of both systems, 3–3–4 and 4–3–3, will show that when two teams play the same 3–3–4 system against each other, each team is left in the same poor defensive situation: a four-man attacking line against a three-man defense. When a 4–3–3 team is up against a 3–3–4 one, this produces four fullbacks to stand up to four forwards, and in attack five forwards against three fullbacks.

But whichever formation is decided upon, the halfback line will be the most important. The most vital member of that line is the center half. The general of the game, this player has to control the entire midfield and coordinate the defense and attack. He will need soccer intelligence as well as excellent athletic ability and must be strong, fast, and preferably tall so that he can command head balls in the middle.

It isn't difficult to understand why the halfback line is often called the "linkmen," for that is what they do—link the defense to the attack and vice versa.

Fullbacks and forwards are easier to define. The forwards must have speed, particularly the wingmen, plus dribbling and shooting skills; the fullbacks, power and reliability.

The Team

Once a team is formed, the players must remember the necessity of keeping their positions and of talking to each other—telling each other to mark a man, to cover a hole in defense, calling out for the ball. A team that talks is one that is learning how to play soccer properly.

Trying to teach a new, young team how to keep position is probably the most frustrating of the basic tactics. Young players have a tendency to chase after the ball; some of them will even cross the field to do it.

One method of correcting this that generally works is to divide the practice field up into sections. This should be done with cones to make four zones. One line of cones will divide the field into two—left and right. The other cones are used to cross-divide it. Only use one of the goals and play a four- or five-man forward line against the defensive section of the team.

The defensive players are placed in their respective zones and told to stay there. If they have the ball in their own zone, they may tackle and dribble around an attacking player, but they are not allowed to cross the line with the ball. It must be passed into another zone. They should be instructed to try and pass between the cones. This will help develop accuracy in passing.

The attacking players should only be allowed to run up and down the field, not across it. A few practice sessions of this should firmly fix in their minds where they should be for most of the time.

Of course, in actual play the zones are not fixed; they

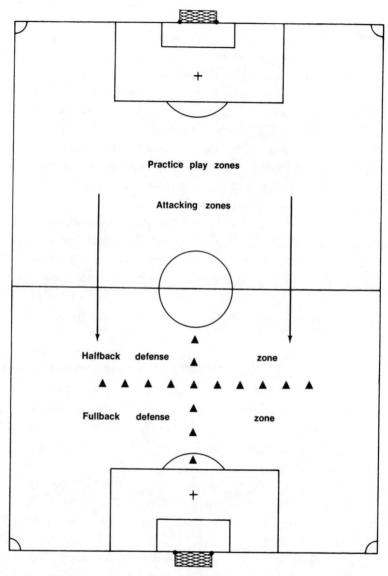

7. Using cones to mark off practice position zones.

change with the flow of the game. Nevertheless, it is essential for players to start off by acquiring the best of habits. A team that gets used to the word *zone* and what it stands for in soccer will be prepared for the years ahead when they will be involved in more complicated zone-play tactics.

The Kick

A youngster who cannot kick the ball properly will never make a good soccer player. Learning the various ways to kick is therefore essential, and nobody, not even the finest professional, ever stops trying to improve his kicking.

Novices usually start off by kicking the ball with the toe, called a "toe-punt." Coaches should firmly discourage this from the outset, even though a player will insist that he can kick farther this way than the proper way. A player will never achieve accuracy or subtlety if he kicks with his toe.

There are three basic methods of kicking:

1. The instep kick
2. The inside foot kick
3. The outside foot kick

THE INSTEP KICK

It may be difficult for a young player to understand at first, but the leg that supports him when he goes to kick the ball is more important than the kicking leg. The reason for this is that what happens to the ball after it has been kicked will be dependent upon the position of the supporting leg.

For instance, the supporting leg is always placed along-

8. The WRONG way to kick the ball. NEVER use the toe.

9. The correct way to approach the ball. The supporting leg should be alongside the ball and about 9 inches away from it. Note that this player kicks with his left foot.

10. The supporting foot is too far back. This will force the weight of the player backward, and when he kicks the ball, it will rise. However, this method of kicking can be taught to goalkeepers and fullbacks who will be taking goal kicks.

11. The supporting foot is too far forward. The ball will bounce along the ground or spin off its intended line of direction.

side the ball. If it is too far back when the kick is taken, the ball will rise. Placed too far forward, the ball will bounce along the ground. (The player may also stub his toe on the ground.)

There are technical, physiological reasons for this. The leg is like two levers, the upper thigh being one and the lower calf the other. In order to use the power of these levers to the best advantage, the knee, which provides the moving joint between them, must be over the top of the ball when it is kicked. To accomplish that, the supporting leg has to be alongside the ball at the time of impact. Basically, it is a question of the correct ratio between stance, weight distribution, and maximal muscle alignment.

In order to produce a straight kick, the ball has to be

struck at its center by the instep, the flat part of the shoe where it is laced. Striking it on one side will produce a curve—something an older player will learn to do deliberately as he progresses.

Once the kicking foot has struck the ball, it must follow through the line of flight. This is to provide added power and accurate direction. The player's eye, on the ball all the time, should follow the ball's flight.

The kick must be made in one fluid motion—concentration is vital. Once the player has mastered this kick he will be able to go on to chip shots, curve shots, roundhouse kicks, and so on. But before all of that, he *must* develop a powerful instep kick to the point where it becomes second nature to him.

12. The powerful follow-through. Note the kicker's eye should be on the ball at all times. The approach, kick, and follow-through should be done in one continual, fluid motion.

INSIDE AND OUTSIDE KICKS

These kicks are used for short passing and, as their names indicate, they are taken with either the outside or inside of the foot.

Players are often surprised at the power they can get into these kicks, but more than power, they can be used to great effect because they can be made with speed. The inside kick should be done with either a stroking motion or an abrupt, snapping motion. Circumstances will dictate which method is used; the less time there is to make the pass, the more concise the move. The body should be forward, over the ball.

The outside kick is also called a flick kick because when the outside of the foot strikes the ball, the action is rather like flicking the foot away. When a player makes an outside foot pass, his body, for once, should be leaning back, away from the ball. The knee should lead, with the ankle following, producing a whiplike action.

Once a player has mastered the three basic kicking styles, he has his soccer artillery ready. It won't be long before he discovers that an instep kick has more variations than the low drive.

Using the same approach but varying the striking zone on the ball will produce a different effect. For instance, a shoe striking low on the ball will make it rise; striking to one side will produce a curve. Striking low but with the kicking foot suddenly held back—no follow-through—will produce a chip shot.

The enjoyment of these shots, though, will not be realized until the player has absolute mastery of the basic skills

13. The inside foot kick. Used mainly for short, sharp passes. The body weight should be forward and the knee over the ball.

14. The outside foot kick (sometimes called the flick kick). The body should be leaning back from the ball. The knee leads with the ankle following, and in so doing produces the flick action.

of kicking. It is advisable for young players to resist the temptation of moving on to the other, more advanced forms of kicking until the fundamental techniques have become instinctive.

Players, quite naturally, like to show off their abilities and to many of them the flashy-looking kick, like a bicycle or scissors kick, is the thing they want to master most. Wonderful as the bicycle kick is to see when it is performed properly, it rarely scores goals.

Trapping

To trap the ball means to bring it under control. It is an essential skill because without it a player will not get possession of a bouncing ball.

There are two fundamental methods: the foot trap and the body trap. Beginners will find both methods difficult at first.

The best way to practice the foot trap is with two players. One player throws the ball in the air to the other. The receiving player should be alert and keep his eye on the ball. As it comes down to the ground, the foot should be raised slightly, then at the instant the ball hits the ground, it should be covered, gently, with the sole of the shoe.

As the foot traps the ball, the ankle should be relaxed. The player should not attack the ball; the object is to tame it and bring it under immediate control. Although it is desirable for players to become two-footed, this does take time, and beginning players will either be left- or right-foot dominant. (The majority will be right-footed.) The left-footed player

15. Trapping. The player's eyes are looking directly up at the ball, his foot is poised, *not raised up in the air.*

16. His foot goes to cover the ball. The ankle should be relaxed.

17. The trap has been completed and the ball is under control.

traps with his left foot. This is correct, since once the ball has been trapped and is under control, it has to be either passed or dribbled, and these movements usually start by kicking the ball with the dominant foot.

The body trap should also be practiced by two players, but the throw should be lower—in baseball terms a high-line drive instead of a pop-up.

The player trapping the ball should move his arms away from his body. This is done for two reasons: first, so that the ball does not touch the hands or arms, in which case the referee would probably call a "handball" foul; and second, to help to make the chest concave and, therefore, a hollow cushion. The ball should be taken on the chest; it will then

18. The player receives the ball on his chest. Note that the arms should be away from the body, protecting against a "handball" foul and helping to make the chest concave.

19. The ball falls off the concave chest to the ground, where it can be easily controlled by the feet.

bounce softly down to the ground, where it can be controlled by the foot.

Mastering these techniques will make a player feel at ease with the ball. He will start building up a rapport that, as he progresses, will lead to an instinctive, confident relationship between his body and the ball. This is what makes a good soccer player.

Once the foot and body traps become second nature to a player, he will develop other more sophisticated methods of trapping the ball, such as using the inside of the knee or even "catching" the ball in the instep of his shoe. But before all the fancy moves, he must become absolutely proficient in the basic means of controlling a high-moving ball.

Passing

A team that does not learn how to pass properly will not win many games. In theory the principle of passing is simple: just play "keep away" until the team scores a goal. However, if "keep away" was all that was necessary, the game would become boring. In any event, a team will seldom be able to pass all the way to the goal, mainly because there is another team in the way. Nevertheless, without passing ability a soccer team is not a team at all, just eleven players kicking a ball around.

Over the years there have been different ideas about the kinds of passing that are most successful. The English once used the long pass over the heads of the opposing halfbacks to their own forward line. The Italians then developed the short, sharp pass. A combination of the two is the ideal. It just depends on the circumstances.

In any country where soccer is the national sport, you will almost certainly see, maybe in a back alley, a boy kicking a ball up against a wall. This apparently aimless pastime is possibly the basis of some of the finest soccer-passing tactics in the game. Substitute the wall for another player on the soccer field, and the backstreet kick-about becomes a deadly goal-making play.

An excellent way of learning the wall pass and many other tactics is to have a soccer backboard constructed. A soccer backboard is the soccer variation of a tennis backboard. The preferred dimensions are 12 feet high by 30 feet long. It should be made of heavy planks of hardwood and be supported by bolted uprights set onto piers. Once the backboard is up, imaginary goalposts should be painted on it—8 feet high by 24 feet long—plus marked-off areas 6 feet in from the goalpost uprights.

A valuable advantage of the backboard is that players can practice on their own. The ball should bounce back toward

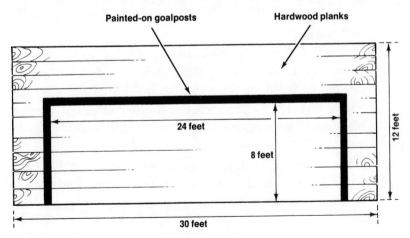

20. A rough plan of a soccer backboard.

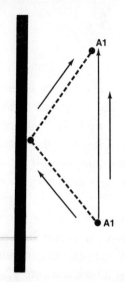

21. How a player should practice rebounding the ball off the backboard. He will have to sprint quite quickly to catch up to and receive the ball as it comes off the wall. As well as teaching the principles of the wall pass, the backboard is invaluable for a player to learn, on his own, how to control the ball.

the player instead of landing somewhere behind a real goal; the only time nets are left up on goals is during game periods. The immediate purpose of the backboard, however, is for players to learn how the wall pass works and why it works so well.

A line of players should stand a few feet away from the board and at an angle. In turn, each one sends off a pass toward the board; he must then sprint forward to collect the angled rebound. As proficiency improves, he should increase his distance from the board.

Once the technique has been mastered, it should be practiced on the field in groups of three—two attackers and one defender. Attacker number one makes the initial pass to attacker number two when he is pressed by the defender. The

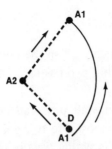

22. The single wall pass. Player A1 is being pressed by a defending player, so he passes the ball to "the wall," only this time the wall is one of his own men—A2. This player rebounds the ball—passes it—behind the defending player where it is collected by A1, who has sprinted around player D.

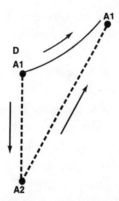

23. The back pass. Another version of the wall-pass tactic is the back pass. Player A1 is being attacked by a defending man, so he passes back to "the wall," player A2. Again the ball rebounds at an angle, and player A1 sprints into a position to collect. In all wall-pass plays it is important to remember that the player who makes the first pass must move very quickly, the second he has kicked the ball, toward his new position so that he can collect the rebounding ball.

players should immediately grasp the point of the backboard training. Attacker number two has taken the place of the wall and rebounds the ball.

While this type of wall pass can be used almost anywhere on the field, it is most effective going down the wings. The main reason for this is that usually the "wall" man has his back to the sideline and will not be tackled from behind.

Having mastered the first wall pass, players are ready for a variation called the back pass. The principle is exactly the same: an attacker is being pressed by a defender. This time he "backs" the ball off the wall. Attacker number two rebounds (passes) the ball forward to a sprinting attacker number one.

One thing that will be very quickly learned is that other players are not as reliable as the backboard. The backboard does not move, and it will always rebound the ball. But this is something that has to be learned, for without accurate passing, games will not be won.

The longer the pass, the more chance it has of being intercepted. Accurate, short passes will win games. It is very tempting for a player who is capable of kicking long to crash the ball upfield at every opportunity. This isn't helped by spectators shouting their approval from the sidelines. Chances are the ball will land up at the feet of an opposing player.

Possession of the ball is how soccer games are won. Make a note of the number of times the long kick is wasted. The strong kick has its place, but it is usually when the kicker has no alternative but to just get rid of the ball at all costs.

When passing techniques are being learned, players should make a point of "calling for the ball." The action on a soccer field is generally fast—if it isn't, something is wrong—and players who are in open positions and near the play should literally call out for the ball.

Heading

When spectators see a player make a terrific head shot, particularly if it is a high one, they wonder if it hurts. Well, the answer is that if it isn't done properly, yes, it does. The research of medical centers, both in Europe and the United States, indicates that the impact from a hard soccer ball on the head is similar to a boxer receiving a punch to the head.

As the ability of young, inexperienced players to control heading techniques will not be all that great, it seems advisable for them *not* to be overenthusiastic with their heading.

There is only one way to head a ball and that is to use the center of the forehead and at the same time to tense the neck muscles. If the ball strikes a player on the top of his head, he will probably end up with a headache.

"*Never* let the ball hit you" is the rule. It should always be "punched" with the forehead. The eyes must be open and on the ball all the time, although at the moment of impact the eyes will, of course, blink. The direction of the ball off the head will depend on the angle at which it is struck.

The best method of practicing is for the team to form a circle with one player or the coach in the middle. The middle man throws the ball at each player, who should head it back to his waiting hands. Then the player should move his neck

24. The proper way to head the ball. Use the center of the forehead, tense the neck muscles, and punch at the ball. Never just let the ball hit the head.

and head downward slightly so that he punches the ball toward the feet of the man in the middle of the circle.

To accomplish the downward head, a player often has to jump so that his head is higher than the ball when it is struck.

By using this method, the player will get the feel of the head ball and begin to understand how he can control its direction from his head to another player. Also, with more experience, the less frightened a player will be, and therefore less likely to be hurt.

The most dramatic use of the head is on the corner shot, usually a ball that comes in a high arc into the goalmouth. The technique is for the forward to jump up toward the ball and head it either into the corner of the net or downward to the ground. (Hence the practice sessions.) The second maneuver, although more difficult to do, is generally more effective because the goalkeeper is looking for the high head shot.

An even more dramatic head is the dive, again often taken from a corner kick. The body should be parallel to the ground with the head firmly pushed forward so that it strikes the ball as it comes into target range.

A word of caution: *do not* try to head a low ball when other players are in the close vicinity. One player may go to kick what to him is a high ball while the other player may go to head what to him is a low ball. Sometimes the foot and head meet. It is of little consequence that the referee will call a free kick for "high kicking" if you have had a foot in your face.

It is amazing, especially among younger players, what happens when one of them heads a high ball. Naturally, the ball always goes back up into the air, and another player

—usually from the other team—will have a go at it. Back it will come, and off we go again until some bright player traps the ball and brings it under control and into his possession.

To repeat the rule for young players: if in doubt, don't head; trap.

Tackling

If defensive players do not know how to tackle effectively, then a team to all intents and purposes will have no defense. And if there is no defense, there will be a poor attack because defenders have to gain possession of the ball in order to pass it upfield to the halfbacks and/or forwards. A team can quite easily evaluate its defense by noting how it scores its goals. If most are made on dramatic breakaways, it means an ineffectual defense.

While good positioning is essential, that alone will not give a player the ball. The essence of good tackling is timing. Most beginners think of tackling as rushing headlong in the hope of kicking the ball away from the attacking player. They usually end up on the ground while the attacker heads for goal. Tackling is a cat-and-mouse game, with the defender being the cat.

Beginning with position, the defender should always stand between the goal and the player he is marking. When the ball is passed to the marked player, the defender then has the opportunity of intercepting the ball before it reaches the attacker.

25. The cat and mouse. The defender as the cat. It is far better to wait until the attacker makes a mistake before committing oneself to a tackle.

26. The defender has decided it is right to move in and strike. Close to the attacker and using the side of his foot, with his body weight moving forward and his forward leg taking the weight, he leans in and strikes.

27. The correct way to make a sliding tackle. Note that the tackler's foot strikes at the ball. If the referee decides the tackler played the man and not the ball, he will call for a free kick.

If an attacker is approaching a defender, the first objective is to try and force the attacker toward the touchline. (The nearer he is to the touchline, the less immediate danger.) This is done by stalking the player and moving in aggressively but without attempting to tackle.

Hustling an attacker can force him into making a mistake, such as allowing the ball to run too far in front of him. Then is the time to strike. When a defender does strike, it has to be with authority. But he must not try to take the ball away from the attacker. Instead, he must first block the ball.

Under no circumstances should a player stick his leg out when he tries to make a tackle. The full weight of the body must be behind the blocking move. Sticking a leg out in a feeble attempt at a tackle can result in a badly kicked ankle, or worse.

The practice drill is done with two players, one trying to dribble the ball past the other. The essential factor is for the defending player to learn not to rush in but to stalk.

When the players become proficient at this one-on-one drill, they should move on to three attackers and two defenders. Here good marking combined with aggressive maneuvering will teach them the art of anticipation. One man stalks while the other tries to anticipate when and where the pass will come. He learns to use and control the available space, which is the element of good defensive marking.

A note about the sliding tackle, which is basically a running tackle made from the side. Many players use this tackle to very good effect, but it does take superb timing; otherwise, it will result in a foul. A referee must determine which the defender struck first, the ball or the man. For this reason, it is better to concentrate on the blocking move until a player is confident and experienced enough to be able to handle the advanced play.

Dribbling

Sooner or later every player on the field except the goalkeeper will have to dribble. Traditionally, it is the forwards, or strikers, who are called on to dribble most. There is always some danger in dribbling, in that the player may lose the ball. This is why it is unwise for fullbacks to make a practice of it; their job is to clear the ball upfield, either by short passing to their halfbacks, or by kicking up the wings.

Dribbling is actually two things—moving the ball with the inside or outside of the foot, and feinting with the body without actually touching the ball with the foot.

All good dribblers have excellent ball control and balance. Balance is almost as important as skill with the ball.

The standard drills for dribbling are simple. A series of cones should be set out—about a yard apart from each other (in the same way as they are set up for the tryouts). The player has to weave between them without knocking them over. He should be sure to keep the ball as close to his foot as possible, only a matter of inches in front. His body should sway as he makes his way through the cones. From this he will learn balance and control.

Next, the player should go down the field pushing the ball from one foot to the next. This will look rather like a dance, but it will teach him how to use the balls of his feet and how to keep proper balance by keeping his weight forward in a crouching stance.

Feinting is a vital part of the dribble, and it should be first learned without the ball. Two players should face each other. One should be the attacker, the other the defender. The attacker has to initiate the moves. First the attacker suddenly moves in one direction, then another. The defender has to react quickly as if he were trying to cut the attacker off. The great Stanley Matthews was a master at feinting, and he would leave defenders standing, sometimes even lying, on the ground as he weaved past them.

The next step is performing the same practice drill with the ball. The attacker has to learn that he can sway in one direction but actually push the ball, then himself, in the other. Variation of speed is essential. Sudden, quick bursts of speed will fool a defender.

A player who tends to be a good dribbler will always

28. Dancing down the field with the ball. The player punts the ball from one foot to the other. This is also, incidentally, an excellent conditioning exercise.

check his opponent's leg dominance in the first few minutes of the game. It is easier to make a successful dribble on the weak side of a player than on his dominant side. For example, if a left-winger was approaching the right back, he would probably have more success going to the back's left side. (This would be inside the player and toward the goal.) The main reason for this is because the attacker will be passing on the defender's supporting-foot side, and he will tend to catch the defender off balance.

There are two basic dribbles and/or feints that players should learn. The first one covers any player who is going down the outside, the wing. Usually he will have a halfback or back running alongside of him. He must judge the timing, stop and pull the ball back, immediately cut inside the defender, and head toward the goal.

The second tactic is used when approaching a defender. The attacker should feint to one side of the defender, then speed around the other side of him. But in doing so, he kicks the ball on the opposite side of the player running to collect it from behind the man.

A variation of this tactic is to wait for the opening, and then punt the ball along the ground through the defender's legs, again racing around the player to collect the ball from behind him.

The Throw-in

What players often seem to forget is that taking a throw-in gives them an attacking advantage. To start with, they have possession of the ball—the name of the game—and if they are intelligent, the start of a tactic.

29. The pass ball. The ball goes one way, the player the other. It is important that the attacker feints going one way before he kicks the ball.

30. He will then race around the defender to pick up behind him.

31. A variation of the pass ball. Many defenders approach an attacker with their legs open. At the right moment the attacker punts the ball through the defender's open legs.

32. Again he races around the defender to collect the ball behind him. He has beaten his man.

It is amazing how many players seem unable to make a proper throw-in. It's a very simple move, and with exceptional players it can be a devastating one.

First the basic rule: a throw-in is given when the ball is put out of play over the touchline. It is the linesman's job to call throw-ins, and he will award them *against* the team that put the ball out.

To make a throw-in, both feet must be on the ground at the moment the ball is released, the ball must be held in two hands, and the throw must originate from the back of the head. The feet must either be on or behind the line when the throw is made.

There are two ways of approaching the move; one is speed, which means the player nearest the ball picks it up and throws it to the nearest unmarked player on his team. The other is the set-piece play using the long throw. This is usually taken by a halfback or wingman.

Wings and halfbacks (sometimes called winghalfs) should spend more than the average time practicing their throw-ins and developing the long throw. A respectable distance, for an Under-12 player, would be 50 feet.

Remember that a player cannot be offside from a throw-in.

On the long throw it is a good ploy for an attacking player to stand near the thrower, calling for the ball. Both of them know where the throw is to go, but this tactic must force at least one defender to be deployed to mark the man calling out.

When marking on a throw-in, defenders must follow the rule of always placing themselves *behind* an attacker. If they

33. The standard throw-in. The ball comes from behind the head, firmly grasped in two hands. The legs are together and the feet are behind the line. Both feet must be on the ground when the throw is made.

don't do this, the ball will go over their heads, and the attacker will be away free.

Naturally, there are many other throw-in plays, and you can invent your own if you wish. But all of them depend on a player who knows how to throw the ball properly. It will be a total waste of effort if on the most spectacular play, the thrower lifts his back leg as he lets go of the ball. The throw is then given to the other side.

The Corner Kick

A corner kick is awarded when a defending player is the last to touch the ball when it goes out of play over his own team's goal line. Very often it is the goalkeeper who does this while making a save. A corner kick is then awarded the attacking team, and the kick is taken from the corner arc closest to where the ball crossed the line. A goal may be scored directly from a corner kick.

Note that there is no offside from a corner kick.

In a close game between professional teams, it is amazing how often the deciding goal comes from either a corner kick or a free kick. Therefore, the tactics used are very important.

There are two basic ways of handling the play. The first and most popular is for the wingman to kick the ball in an arc so that it travels up into the penalty area close to the goalmouth. The object is for an attacking forward to then head the ball into the net.

The other method is the short kick, which we'll go into later.

Obviously, the best way to practice the long kick is for two players to go out on a field. One takes the kick, and the other stands by the goalmouth presenting his head as a target. A wise coach sees to it that the tallest forwards are standing by the goal to try for the head.

Once a player is proficient in taking routine corners, he can move on to something more sophisticated—the out-swinger or the in-swinger.

In professional soccer it is presumed that most forwards are two-footed, that is, they can kick just as well with either foot. But this is not a common skill with beginners. The outcome is that most amateur corner kicks are out-swingers. This means that as the left-winger takes the left-wing corners and the right-winger the right ones, their natural movements and kicks will impart a slight spin (English) to the ball. The spin will tend to carry the high ball away from the goalmouth. This is fine, of course, provided the attacking line is in the right place to get to the ball.

An excellent way to reverse this is for the left player to take the right-field corners and vice versa. What happens then is that the ball comes high over the penalty area in an in-swing toward the far upright of the goal. (This is often called a banana kick.) The best German teams are experts at the in-swinging corner kick.

The tallest player should be positioned to get a good head to the ball. Occasionally, this kind of kick will be so well taken that a goal will be scored directly from it, and that is a very exciting moment.

The short corner kick requires two players, one to take the kick, the other to receive it short and then either chip the

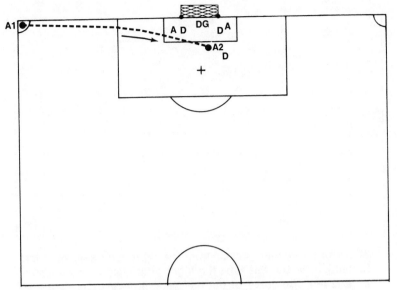

34. The out-swinger. A corner kick taken from the left side of the field by a left-footed kicker. He will impart a natural spin, which will tend to take the ball away from the goalmouth.

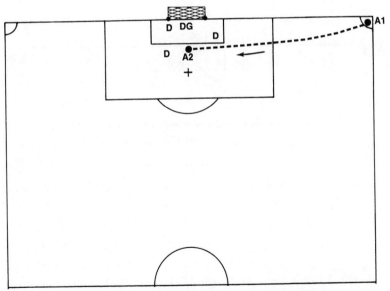

35. The in-swinger. A corner kick taken from the right side of the field but by a left-footed kicker. He will impart the same natural spin this time, but the kick will tend to curve the ball inward toward the goalmouth.

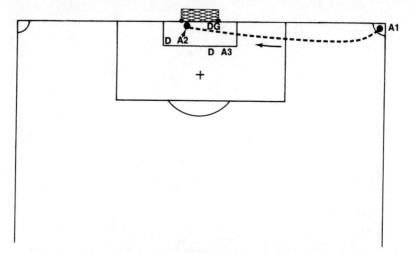

36. The in-swinger, kicked from the right-hand side by a left-footed kicker, but this time the flight of the ball is much less of an arc, and the curve of the ball takes it very close to the far upright of the goal. The attacking center forward would rush forward in an attempt to head the ball home. Very occasionally the corner kicker makes his own goal using this type of in-swinger.

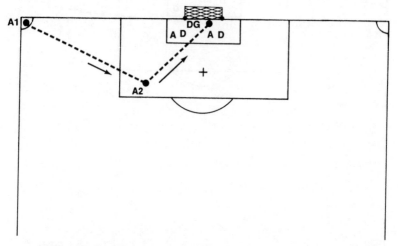

37. The short corner. Player A1 is taking the kick and player A2 positions himself just inside the penalty area. Other attacking players position themselves in what would be the most usual places on the field for a long kick. The kick is made as a ground pass and A2 shoots for goal.

ball into the goalmouth to another player or take a shot himself. Very often it is wise for two players to be in the receiving positions because an alert defense will send players over to mark the short receiver.

Whichever kick is used, it is always a good ploy for a halfback to be in the short receiver position even though the team knows the kick is to be a long one. This should draw a defender away from the goalmouth to mark the man, and the fewer defenders in the goalmouth the better. At the same time it is very common for a loose ball to come out of a corner-kick scramble, and a man standing away from the play can often get off a good shot at goal.

The Free Kick and the Penalty

There are two kinds of free kick, direct and indirect, and they are awarded against the team that commits a foul.

Basically, the nine fouls for which a referee will award a direct kick are physical ones, such as tripping, kicking an opponent, charging in a dangerous manner, hand ball, and so on. Indirect kicks are given for intentional obstruction, such as high kicking.

A direct kick means that a goal can be scored directly by the player taking the kick. An indirect kick means the ball must be touched or be played by another player before a goal can be scored. In neither case can the kicker touch the ball twice until it has been played by another man.

The tactics to employ will depend on where the foul takes place. If it is in midfield, the quicker the kick is taken the better, because the attacking team then has an important element of surprise going for it. If the foul takes place well in the defending team's half, then a prearranged play can be set up. The purpose of the setup play is to take the defenders by surprise. They know the ball is going to come toward their goal; the question is how and where.

The usual defense against a free kick that is within 20 yards of the goal is for the goalkeeper to arrange his defense in a wall. The purpose is to obscure part of the goalmouth, leaving the goalkeeper to guard the open part. One weakness of this defense is if the attacking team has a kicker who can put a power shot over the heads of the wall. Incidentally, it is advisable for the defenders to cover their groins with their hands.

Different teams will, of course, use different tactics with direct and indirect kicks, but when they are close to the defending goal, it is worthwhile to consider using the same type of play irrespective of whether the foul is direct or indirect. Of course, if a team does have a fantastic striker, he should try on a direct.

A penalty kick is awarded when a direct kick infringement takes place in the penalty area. All players must be lined up outside the penalty area and be at least 10 yards from the ball. Only the player taking the kick and the goalkeeper are involved in this play. The goalkeeper must stand on the goal line between the goalposts, and he may not move until the ball has been kicked.

In theory no player should miss a penalty, no matter how good a goalkeeper he faces. Ideally, the kick should be no higher off the ground than 3 feet as it goes just inside one of the goalposts. Accuracy, not power, is the most important element here.

A team should always know before a game which of their players will take penalty kicks if the occasion arises. There is no rule that says it has to be one of the forwards. Very often the center half or a fullback has an excellent penalty drive.

The player taking the kick must decide where the kick is to be aimed *before* his run at the ball. There is no need for trickery. His eye should be on the ball—some goalkeepers watch the kicker's eyes just before the kick to get a clue as to where the ball will go. The kick should be a solid, rising line shot, and there you will have it—a goal.

Free-Kick Tactics

The most commonly used tactic for taking an indirect free kick is to have two attacking players standing close to each other. One taps the ball in front of the other, who with a short run lets off a shot at goal.

Another variation, and one that is fun, too, involves three attacking players and a little bit of playacting. Two players stand close to each other apparently discussing which of them will take the kick. Naturally, the defense will be keeping a close eye on them. Suddenly one of the attackers runs at the ball, but instead of kicking it he jumps over it. The second player quickly passes the ball across field to the third player, who lets off a shot at goal.

Obviously, there are many plays to try, but it is advisable, particularly with younger players, to keep things as simple as possible. The main thing is that the players know exactly what to do in all circumstances. This means constant practice and good communications.

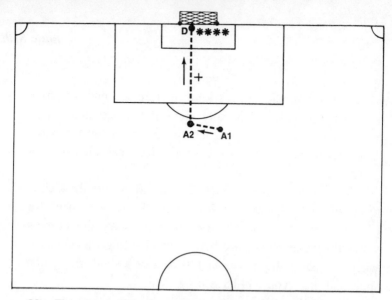

38. The standard indirect free-kick ploy. Attacker A1 makes a short pass a few feet in front of attacker A2. A2 blasts a shot between the goalkeeper and the defensive wall.

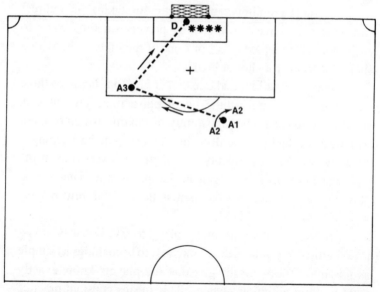

39. A variation on the indirect free-kick ploy. This one can be fun to do and involves a small amount of playacting. Attacking player A1 stands, apparently discussing the kick with A2. A2 runs at the ball, then over it. A1 makes a ground pass to player A3, who has been standing idly just inside the penalty area. He comes to life and puts a power shot between the keeper and the wall.

Penalty Tactics

Once it has been decided which players are capable of taking good penalty kicks, they should go off on their own to practice.

If a club has been lucky enough to have a soccer kickboard constructed, here is another way it can be put to good use. Mark the board with two vertical lines, each 6 feet in from the uprights. Soccer balls should be painted on as targets inside these areas. Mark off a penalty spot, 12 yards from the goal line. Penalty-kick players can then practice taking shots at the targets.

On the face of it, the penalty kicker has all the advantages. The goalkeeper is not allowed to move his feet until the ball has been kicked. (If he does move his feet, the kick is retaken.) The kick is a relatively short one, 12 yards, and with the ball properly placed, on target, it is virtually impossible to save.

But penalty kicks are sometimes missed. With a calm player who has a good, accurate kick, the outcome is assured—a goal.

Goalkeeping

The most difficult position to fill on a new soccer team is the goalkeeper. Lots of youngsters like the idea of playing in goal, and they should try it. They will begin to understand the difficulties involved, and they may discover that they have a natural talent. But of all the positions in soccer, the one that allows for the least mistakes is the goalkeeper. Forwards can miss shots at goal and everyone will sigh, but a goalie's mistake usually means a goal allowed.

Ideally, the potential goalkeeper should be fairly tall and athletic. His hands should be on the large side and his serious ambitions toward playing-out, zero. The first lesson to be learned is that no shot at goal is an easy save. The margin for error is too great to allow for complacency.

The only way for a goalie to start a training program is to let other players try to score off him. He will need experience at ground shots, high shots, corner kicks, and heads. If possible, he should always have a backup to his hands. This means his trunk and legs should always be behind the ball so that if it slips out of his hands, it will hit some other part of him.

When a goalkeeper goes to get a ground ball, he should either stand with his legs together and bend down to pick up the ball, or he should go down to the ground on one knee with his other leg almost at right angles to it, thus filling the hole between his legs. Whichever method is used, the rule is to gather the ball to the body.

The exception to this is the high ball; obviously, there is no part of the body that can be used as backup here. This is when the hands must be sure and safe—one reason for having a goalie with big hands.

Anticipation is a vital prerequisite for good goalkeepers. They must be alert to the play going on out in the field at all times and able to judge where the ball is going to come from, whether it will be shot at the goal, or be a pass across the goalmouth to an advancing forward.

If at any time the goalie is not confident that he can catch the ball, he must punch or deflect it away. Punching should be done with two fists, side by side. They present a larger surface and they help to avoid straining the wrists.

40. Going for a ground ball. Standing with the legs together—if they were apart, the ball could go through them into the goal—the keeper bends forward to collect the ball.

41. The keeper then gathers the ball to his body. Notice how the hands are firmly clasped under the ball, hugging it to the body.

42. An alternate way to gather a ground ball. Again the leg, this time kneeling, protects the space. If the keeper does fail to hold the ball, at least it will bounce off him, and there is still a chance it will not end up in the back of the net.

The goalkeeper is in charge of the defense line, if for no other reason than he has the best view of the field. He must call out to his backs to fill spaces in the defense, to cover attacking forwards, and to call for the pass back to him if a defensive player is being pressed.

Once the goalkeeper has possession of the ball, he is in a fine position to start an attack. He has the choice of where to send the ball either by kicking it or throwing it. For instance, if he knows that the attacking team has a strong left wing but a weak right wing, then naturally he should send the ball up the right wing to one of his own halfbacks.

43. Here the goalie leaps for a high ball. This save was in fact made after he had already made one save, but an alert forward took a second shot. Notice how the hands are behind the ball.

44. As the goalie falls to the ground, he hugs the ball to his body. This technique can also be used when diving across the goalmouth for ground shots.

45. Punching the ball that comes in too high to be safely caught. Both hands form fists, and placing them side by side —this avoids straining the wrists and provides a larger punching surface—the goalie punches clear over the bar.

46. Leaping to gather a cross shot. Again the goalie makes certain that he hugs the ball into his body.

The most controversial play a goalkeeper has to make, particularly from a spectator's point of view, is coming out of his goal to face an attacking player. This happens when there is a breakaway. A single forward has the ball and is running full pelt toward goal. There is no question about it—this is when the goalkeeper rushes out of his goal toward the attacker.

The only drawback to this, and there is no alternative, is if the attacking forward has the ability to chip the ball over the goalie's head. One safeguard, and this isn't always possible, is for a fullback to race into the goalmouth. Although he is not allowed to touch the ball with his hands (without giving away a penalty), he might be able to kick or head it away and so avert a goal.

A goalkeeper is a special player, for he is the last line of defense.

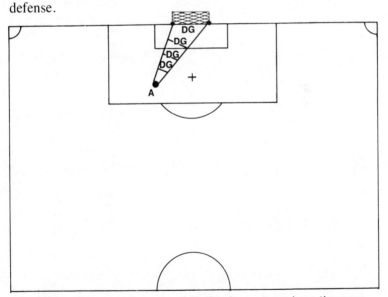

47. The goalkeeper has one objective here: to reduce the area of unguarded goal. It is a simple matter of geometry. He does it by reducing the angle. If a player shoots when the goalie is on the goal line, he has the entire area to choose from, but the closer the goalie gets to the attacker, the narrower the angle and goal space available.

ADVANCED SKILLS

Kicking

If a boy has been playing soccer for at least a season, he should be able to perform the basic forms of kicking, that is, the instep kick and the inside and outside foot kicks. And if he has any ambition, he should have developed other ways of kicking from experience.

Now is the time, however, when he must learn to use the various other kicking techniques correctly.

THE CHIP SHOT

The purpose of the chip shot is to put the ball in the air, in a specific direction, over a short range. It is used mainly for passing, and for placing the ball in the goal area so a forward can collect it and make a shot.

When the kick is made, the supporting foot should be slightly back of the center of the ball (unlike the instep kick, where it is alongside the ball), the kicking foot striking the ball well below its middle line. (If the field is damp, the foot may even take a piece of turf out of the ground.) The kick is made with a stabbing action, so that there is no follow-through. The whole process will make the ball rise and give

48. Chipping the ball. The supporting leg is back of center of the ball. The kicking foot strikes the ball well below its middle in a stabbing action. There should be no follow-through. The ball will then rise with backspin.

49. The standard roundhouse volley. The body is leaning away from the ball so as to generate as much power as possible. The power comes from the knee and below. Here as the ball falls, the kick will be made.

it a backspin so that it will tend to stay put when it lands, instead of rolling away.

The chip shot works best when the ball is still or coming toward a player as he goes to make the kick. If the ball is moving away from him when he attempts a chip, it will be very difficult to produce backspin, and the result will be an undisciplined long pass.

THE VOLLEY

A volley involves kicking the ball while it is in the air. A half-volley occurs when the ball is struck just as it hits the ground. The side-volley, sometimes called a roundhouse kick, is the most effective, and is usually made by a player in a forward position taking a shot at goal.

The principle to keep in mind is that the higher the ball when it is struck, the less the power behind the foot. To compensate for this without losing his speed, the player should lean sideways, away from the ball. To generate the most power, the kicking foot must swing from the knee. Timing is vital, since if the kick is made too early, the ball will go sailing way over the goal.

A variation of the roundhouse volley is the scissors kick. The principles are the same except that the nonkicking leg sweeps forward in the air *before* the ball arrives, in a snapping, scissors action. This generates terrific power to the kicking leg.

THE BICYCLE KICK

The most famous exponent of the bicycle kick was, of course, the great Pelé. But even he rarely scored goals from

50. Going up for the bicycle kick. Note that the kicker throws his nonkicking foot, the right one, into the air first. His eye is zeroed onto the ball, which is coming down from a high bounce.

51. Coming down from the bicycle kick. The kick has been made (in the Pelé fashion with the toe) using the left foot. One arm is already out to take the shock of the fall; as the player continues to fall, he straightens his body and supports himself with both arms. Caution should be used when first trying this kick.

it. Difficult to perform, it has a couple of drawbacks. First, the player lands on his back after he has made the kick. Second, any young player who makes a bicycle kick in a crowded goal area will almost certainly be called for high kicking, which constitutes dangerous play.

The kick is generally made from a high ball that is either bouncing or has come off a player's head. As the ball comes down, the player throws his nonkicking leg into the air along with his body, snaps it back, and then with great force hits the ball with the other leg. The action is a simultaneous, one-two, crossing of the legs in the air.

This is the only kick in soccer which can be taken with the toe—something Pelé preferred to do—but many players use the instep. It is all a question of technique and which type of foot contact works best for the player.

THE BACK-HEEL KICK

As its name implies, this kick is made with the back of the heel, which should strike the ball directly in its center with a sharp, forceful action. Obviously, a player has to be certain before making the kick that there is someone from his own team behind him—and that player should call out for the ball.

Properly executed, the back-heel can be used as a variation of the back-wall pass. It can also be used in an indirect free-kick situation. The player makes the kick and then quickly gets out of the way while his colleague takes a shot.

A further variation is to draw the ball back with the sole of the shoe, making good use of the cleats. It is almost im-

52. The back-heel kick. The ball should be struck firmly and sharply in its center. This is an excellent kick to use for a back pass—provided you have a colleague waiting for it.

53. Using the cleats to pull the ball backward. Little power can be generated here, but the kick is of value as a feint move in avoiding a player or in dribbling.

possible to get any power into the move, so it can only be made over a very short range. Since the move is made as if the player were stepping over the ball, it is a useful feint.

THE CURVE OR SWERVE

Being able to deliberately swerve the ball well will add a valuable skill to a player's kicking artillery. As will be seen later in the section on advanced free kicks, it can be a tremendous goal-scoring tactic.

The kick is made in two ways: as a high curve in the air or as a low curve around a defending player. This means that the approach to the ball and striking area have to vary to suit the intended outcome.

A player who is two-footed, that is, who can kick with equal force using either foot, will obviously be able to make the kick with the foot of his choice. But the majority of players will elect to use their dominant foot.

The high curve can be put to good effect on corner kicks. By this time an experienced player should know how to make a ball rise by leaning back slightly and striking the ball below its center. If the angle of approach is widened, and the ball is struck on the outer left-hand side, it will swerve—in the air—left to right. Kicked on the outer right-hand side, it will swerve right to left.

From this can be seen the difficulty facing a one-footed kicker when he tries to make a high curving shot in the opposite direction to his foot dominance (for example, a left-footed kicker trying to curve the ball high and to the left—meaning having to kick the ball on the outer right-hand side). He has to approach and kick at the ball against his natural

54. The angle of approach to kick a high swerving ball. This technique can be used to take corner kicks. The kicker is going to use his right foot.

55. The ball is struck on the outer right-hand side and below its center. The body is leaning back slightly away from the ball, which will help to provide lift. The ball will curve away from the goal, taken from the right-hand corner flag.

balance, which feels awkward. This is why it was advised in the section on corner kicks for dominant-foot kickers to shift from one side of the wing to the other to produce an in-swinging ball.

All of which is another very good reason for players to develop two-footed kicking ability.

Swerving the ball low over the ground to curve it around a defender is easier to do left and right for single-dominance kickers. The reason is that the best approach is virtually in a straight line. Doing this will help to keep the knee over the ball so its trajectory will be low.

Again, the ball is struck with a powerful short kick, either on the left- or right-hand side, depending on which way the kicker wishes to swerve the ball. When a left-footed

56. Approaching the ball in a straight line will tend to keep its flight low. Note the knee is well over the top of the ball. This kick will make the ball travel in a straight, low trajectory.

57. The broad part of the instep should strike the ball in which-ever side the player chooses to produce the curve. Here the foot hits the right-hand side, which will make the ball curve away to the left.

58. Here the ball is struck on its left side. It will obviously curve away to the right.

kicker is hitting the ball on the right side, his foot will tend to come across the face of the ball. Increasing the angle of approach will increase the curve.

In both the high and the low swerve, the foot should follow through in the direction of the curve, and, of course, a player's eye must be on the ball at all times.

Again, kicking well is the most important element in soccer. Balance, approach, striking the ball in the right place, and finishing with explosive power are the principles that go into making a player who is able to consistently make a power shot, a smoothly executed pass, a cross from the wing, or a goal.

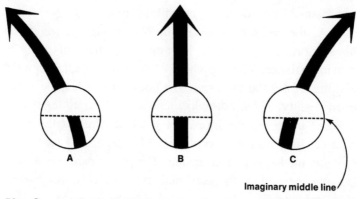

Imaginary middle line

59. Curving the ball. The ball will curve or not curve depending where on its surface it is struck. Kicked as marked in position A, it will obviously curve right to left; position C, left to right. In the center, position B, it will go straight ahead. However, the approach, and again the place it is struck, will also affect its trajectory. Striking low—below an imaginary middle line—will make it rise; striking along a middle line will keep it down.

Trapping and Moving

The player who has learned to trap, to bring a moving ball under control, will quickly realize that after making the trap, he has to do something with the ball—either pass it or move with it—or have it taken away from him.

The trap is only part of a move; very quickly, the player must also decide what he will try to do with the ball when he gets it. This means learning more than the fundamental ways of trapping.

The prettiest-looking trap, but one that can take hours of practicing to master, is to "catch" the ball between the top of the soccer shoe and the lower front calf. Used to control a high ball, it gives a player the opportunity to move his body and change direction while he still has possession.

As the ball comes down, the player puts his weight on his supporting leg, keeping his arms away from his body to provide balance. The trapping foot should be angled upward and the leg bent at the knee. The body will be leaning backward slightly. Then, riding like a punch, the raised leg is then lowered to absorb the impact of the ball while at the same time catching it in the "cup" made by the angled top of the foot and the lower part of the leg. The player can swivel, still keeping the ball in the cup, and move quickly away from close defenders.

Learning this trap will teach a player how to ride with the ball (that is, how to use his body to take the power out of it to cushion its impact). If he presents a nongiving surface, the ball will just bounce off it out of control.

Riding the ball is also essential for the thigh trap, which is used to control a ball coming toward a player a few feet off

60. The first move in an effort to "catch" the ball in the space created between the top of the shoe and the front of the calf. The foot goes up to meet the high-dropping ball.

61. As the ball is caught, the leg is lowered to absorb the impact of the ball.

62. Now the ball is under control and the player can move his body while retaining the ball. The entire action should be done in one fluid motion.

63. Taking the ball, trapping it, on the inside of the thigh. The thigh should move back slightly to absorb the impact of the ball, otherwise it will bounce off the leg and away from the player.

64. Trapping the ball on the top of the thigh. Again the thigh should be lowered as the ball hits it so as to take away the power of the ball. It will then drop down to the feet.

the ground—not high enough to be taken on the chest and too low to control with the foot. The ball is trapped by either the front or the side of the thigh. If the ball strikes the inner part of the raised thigh, the bent leg should move backward to absorb the impact. If it strikes the front of the thigh, the thigh should simultaneously be lowered, thus cushioning the ball so that it drops to the ground in front of the player.

There are times when a player wants the ball to bounce away from him because he is already moving forward to meet it. He can either take it on the chest or the front of the thigh, or if he is really good, on the outside of a raised foot. Which-

65. Again taking the ball on the top of the thigh. This time, though, the player will not drop his thigh to absorb the shock but will allow the ball to bounce off in front of him. He is on the run and wants the ball to roll away so that he can continue in his forward movement.

ever method he adopts, he should know exactly what will happen to the ball—how it will ricochet off the surface he presents.

Trapping is another technique that can be practiced on a soccer backboard. Two players face the board; one of them starts off by kicking the ball at the board. The object is for the other player to use his body—foot, chest, thigh, even buttocks—to bring the rebounding ball under control and then to pass it back to the board.

The better a player becomes at trapping and moving, the more valuable he will be to the team. Trapping is a marvelous way of getting to know the ball and making a friend of it, as Pelé used to say. With continual practice the body and mind will start working smoothly together with confidence and improved ability, in the same way an expert juggler develops a rapport with his twisting, airborne clubs.

Throw-in Tactics

Virtually anyone can take a throw-in. All that is needed is for a player to pick the ball up, follow the rules, and throw it to one of his own men. Why then is it so often misplayed? Probably because it is so easy to do. Yet the proper throw-in can be the first step a team takes toward learning about the use and creation of space.

When taking a throw-in, the opponents have a numerical advantage, so it is important to create space by movement, cunning, and deception. The most important factor is to practice, over and over again, the various predesigned ploys that will be used on the field of play. It is amazing how frequently the same tactics keep on working, even in the same game where the opponents have seen them time after time.

First of all, the throw-in is taken with the whole body, not just the arms. The legs support the torso as it moves forward in a whiplash action, the arms sweeping up and forward, the fingers well splayed out behind the ball. The arms must follow through to give direction and added power.

While speed is often the most important factor in making a throw, it is not always possible (for example, the ball has rolled well out of play, giving the defense time to set up). This is when a little playacting can be brought into action.

For example, suppose it seems that two players are trying to decide who will take the throw. Meanwhile, their colleagues on the field are in constant movement. All of this tends to promote a lack of attention in the defense. Suddenly, one of the men at the line makes a quick throw into an open space—one that an attacker is moving toward. The man is unmarked and is away on the second stage of an attacking maneuver. For such an apparently spontaneous tactic to work, rehearsal is vital.

A more prosaic but nevertheless very effective ploy is the return pass. It should be made with some speed; otherwise the player on the field making the pass will quickly find himself marked by a defender. The player on the line throws the ball either to the head or the feet of his colleague on the field. That player heads or passes the ball directly back to the thrower, who can then either move off down the wing or chip the ball into the center.

Again, the essential element is practice. Surprisingly, players find it difficult to make accurate throws to the head or

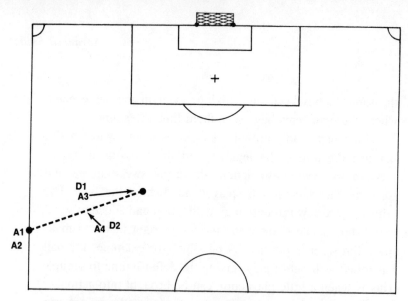

66. The playacting throw-in. Taken when there is time to set up the play. A1 and A2 appear to be arguing about who will take the throw. A3 and A4 keep dancing around, all of which diverts the attention of the defensive players D1 and D2. Suddenly, A1 makes the throw into a space into which A3 runs, thus collecting the ball and heading toward the goal.

feet of other players. Obviously, the drill for them is to practice in pairs. They should vary the distance between themselves as they work at the skill.

Occasionally there will be a player who is capable of making very long throws. If this happens, it is worthwhile for him to make a special effort to increase his ability. The way to do it is to use a medicine ball rather than a soccer ball. The extra weight will build his muscles, and when he goes to throw the lighter soccer ball, the effect can be quite dramatic.

The long throw has many uses. One is when it has to be taken in the defensive half of the field. The thrower and the goalkeeper work in unison. As the throw is about to be made, the goalie runs to the edge of his box, collects the ball, and quickly switches the angle of play by kicking or throwing the

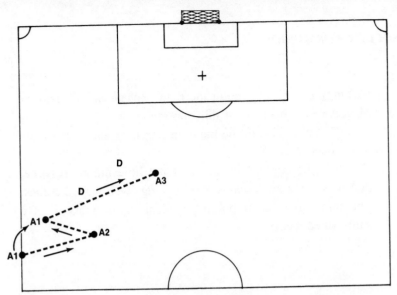

67. The return throw-in. A1 quickly throws to A2, who returns the ball, either with his head or foot. A1 then chips the ball to A3, who is way out in a space all on his own. He can, because he is unmarked, move directly toward the goal area.

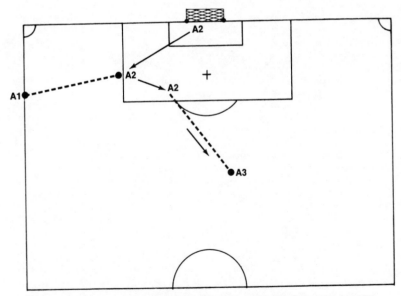

68. The long throw-in taken from the sideline in the defensive area. A1 throws to the goalkeeper, who will, in unison with the throw, move quickly toward the edge of the area. He collects the ball, changes direction, and either kicks or throws it upfield to an awaiting midfielder, A3.

ball up the opposite side of the field. Rehearsal will help the players take advantage of this opportunity.

The throw should be made in one long curve. It should not bounce.

It is the cumulative effect of the little things in soccer that makes for good teams and exciting, well-played games. The throw-in is an important element in the makeup of a well-drilled team.

TACTICS

Creating Space

The wall pass can be the basis of some very successful and simple passing techniques, and as a player advances, this tactic will help him learn how to create and use space.

Look at diagram 69. A1 is being pressed by D3. What does he do? He can try and dribble around D3 or he can pass. If he passes, he has a choice—pass to either A2 or A3.

Naturally, he should opt to pass to A2 because A2 is unmarked and in open space. A3 is being closely marked by D2 so the chances of interception are much greater.

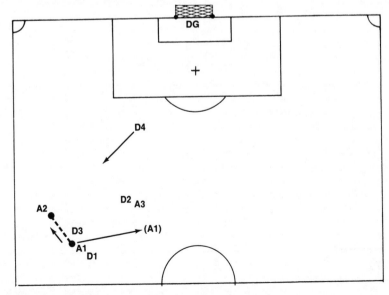

The diagram also shows that A1 does not stand still after having made his pass. It is essential that a player learn the necessity of movement after a pass; this is what gives a game its pace. So A1 moves toward open space.

As an alternate tactic, A2 could pass into the open space behind D2 so that A3 can sprint forward and collect the pass. But this could be dangerous because defender D4 could alter his path and beat A3 to the ball.

The best move is to follow a well-proven soccer principle: if a player has possession of the ball and he has the space, he should move with it.

This is shown in diagram 70. A2 races down the wing, and naturally, D4 moves to tackle him. At the same time, A3 races forward, too, closely marked by D2. Now the classic pass: A2 passes *behind* the defender D4, knowing that A3 will dash forward into the space left open by the defender D4. A3 is away, on his own, racing for goal.

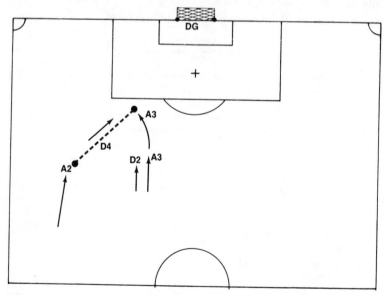

70.

All that has actually happened here is just three simple passes. But it is amazing how seldom all three work to order and in succession. It is also important that player A3 be careful to wait until A2 has kicked the ball forward; otherwise, he stands a chance of anticipating the pass and putting himself in an offside position.

Here, then, is all the justification a player should ever need for acquiring mastery of the basic skills and moves of soccer. If the three attackers involved in the tactic had not learned how to kick and pass the ball properly, the play would have been a disaster.

The Through Pass

Properly executed, the through pass is a tremendous tactic and almost always results in a goal. But it is difficult to pull off, because it requires precision timing, superb use of open space, and a forward who has the ability to make a shot like a bullet.

There is a variation, though, used mainly to overcome the offside trap, that will give a set of attackers the kind of practice needed to make the goal-scoring tactic.

Many teams use the offside game as a defensive ploy, and while it can be very effective, it is also highly vulnerable, particularly if the attacking team has read the game properly. Basically, it consists of moving the fullback line upfield as much as possible, close to the halfway line. This keeps the attacking forwards contained just inside their own half. (You cannot be offside in your own half.)

What then tends to happen is that the forwards, in their

excitement at wanting to tear into all that open space, either anticipate a forward pass and step over the line into an offside position or, because their attention is directed at watching the play going on in their own half, don't realize the backs have crept up on them and drift into an offside position.

Some teams try to use the long ball to beat the tactic. Diagram 71 shows what happens. The ball is lofted over the heads of the fullbacks by A3 and the race is on. Unfortunately for the attacking forwards, the defenders have a few steps advantage. They will usually beat them to the ball and punt it back to their own goalkeeper, who, aware of what is

71.

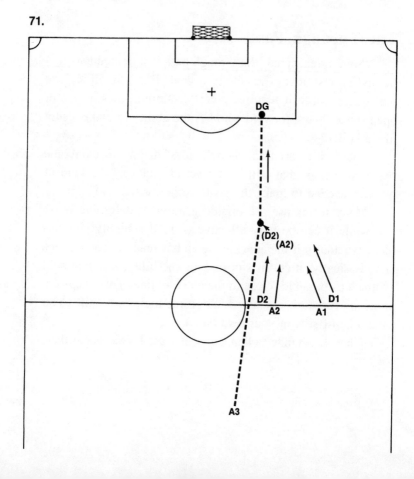

going on, is standing on the edge of the penalty area waiting for the ball.

The way to beat the offside game is really quite simple. All that is needed is some good, short passing and a well-placed ground ball. Diagram 72 shows the means; the outcome will be a defense racing back toward its own goal. This time A3 moves with the ball and then makes a short pass to A2, who in turn puts the ball through the gap. The important factor here is that A1, aware of the ploy, moves immediately after A2 kicks the ball—his timing must be right or he will be offside. The defense will now retreat hurriedly, including the

72.

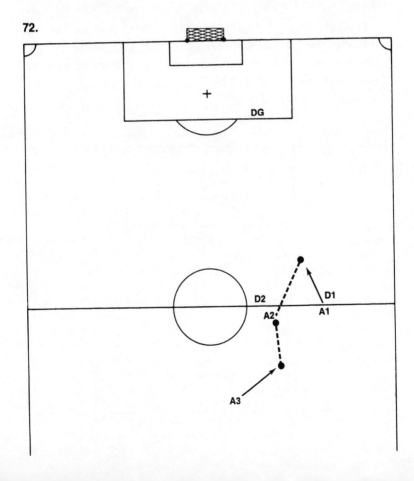

goalkeeper, and the offside tactic will have been broken up.

What the attackers have done is made good use of the through pass to beat the tactic. But, because they are so far from goal, the ploy cannot work to make an immediate score.

As can be seen, it takes three players to set up and make a through pass. When the pass is going to be used to try and score, very often half of the team contributes. It is all a question of preparation.

In diagram 73 presume that A3 is an attacking center half. A1 is tensed and ready. An accurate ground-ball pass is made by A3 to A2. As the defender D3 makes his move to tackle A2, A2 with great precision puts the ball into the gap. Simultaneously, A1 hurls himself forward and on the run smashes the ball into the back of the net. The goalkeeper can see the move taking place, and he, quite rightly, starts to come out of his goal. But he is too late. The through pass has worked perfectly. A goal.

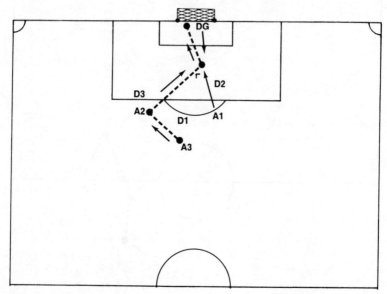

73.

Obviously, this marvelous play doesn't happen on its own. It takes considerable practice, and the three principal players who are to be involved must spend time working together. Apart from the necessity of making accurate passes, timing is the essential factor. Player A1 has to start his run so that he arrives on the ball A2 is setting up for him—too early and the ball will be behind him, too late and the goalkeeper will collect.

There are many other set-piece passing techniques, all of them requiring an imaginative use of space: being able to create it and use it with precision timing. Nevertheless, all of the techniques are derived from the simple principle of passing the ball accurately. Until that fundamental skill has been perfected, the rest is dreaming.

Tactical Defense

The defense has two functions: to stop the opponents from creating a situation from which they can score a goal, and to initiate moves that will result in a successful attack upon the opponents' goal.

First, the ways to defend your own goal.

Again, one starts from the basic formations: a 4–3–3 style of play provides four backs; a 3–3–4, three backs. But, as mentioned before, the abilities of the players should dictate the formation. It will not work having four fullbacks if a team does not have the players who are capable of handling their positions. The old adage, "A chain is as strong as its weakest link," holds true in a defensive soccer line.

For this example, the 4–3–3 formation is used to demonstrate a defensive strategy. Initially, the defense has four men in the backfield. If they are strung out across the field, they will be vulnerable to a series of simple through passes (see diagram 74).

It can be seen how wide open the spaces are behind such a lineup. One good pass and a forward has an open goal facing him. To prevent this, the halfback line has to join the defense, becoming a front line to the fullbacks, who can then be deployed to cover the holes and the errors. Even so, the

74.

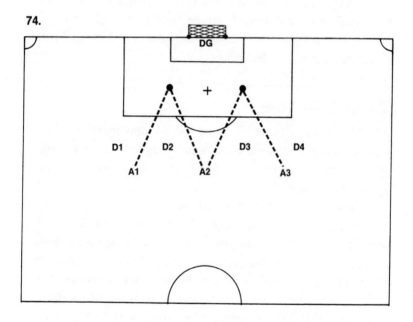

defensive players are probably going to be beaten 50 percent of the time.

One method of setting up the defensive tactical force is shown in diagram 75. Here the four fullbacks have been staggered. D1 and D4 have gone wide with the job of taking on the attacking wingmen. D2 and D3 are tight inside the penalty area to hold up the center of the field. The half-backs—D5, the center half D6, and D7—fill the spaces.

A further variation is shown in diagram 76. This time

75.

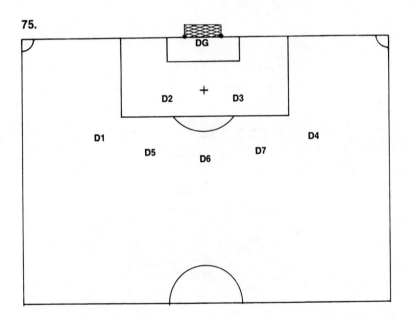

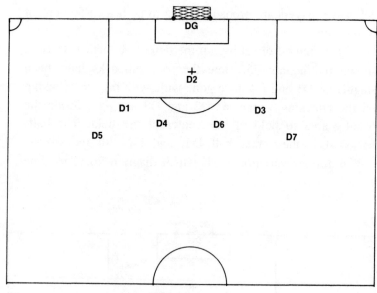

76.

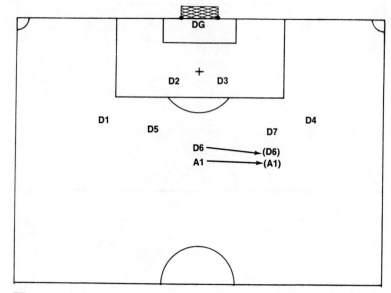

77.

one of the fullbacks is deployed as a backsweeper, or cleanup man (D2), while defenders 1 and 3 cover the outside points of the penalty area. The fourth fullback becomes a second center half with D6 to hold up the middle, and the two half-men, D5 and D7, take on the wings.

Once the most practical method of defensive deployment has been decided on, then the style of marking has to be arranged. There are two systems to choose from: man-to-man and zonal. Most youth teams adopt the man-to-man method, and probably the most common cry from the sidelines during a game is a plea for a back to "mark your man."

The main advantage of the man-to-man system is that a player is given a definite job to do. As the teams line up for the first kickoff, the fullbacks immediately identify their opposite number. For example, the outside left fullback looks down the field to the opposing right wing, traditionally his man.

The principle of man-to-man marking is that the defender follows his opponent wherever he goes. This, of course, can lead to some serious drawbacks. Look at diagram 77. The defensive lineup is the same staggered one shown in diagram 75, where the center of the field is being covered by the halfback line.

The center half D6 would be assigned to mark the opposing center forward A1. But see what happens when A1 moves toward the sidelines. Suddenly, the center of the field is wide-open space. This means that D5, the right halfback, has to move over to fill that space. All that does, of course, is to change the location of the open area.

It could be argued that, as D5 and the other defenders

have their men to mark, too, it will not matter about open spaces because there will not be an unmarked man to penetrate them. In theory and on paper in a diagram this may seem fine, but in a game things do not turn out that way. If they did, then the game would develop into ten groups of two players running around chasing a ball.

What does happen is that an attacker will defeat a defender, and this is the major reason, in a man-to-man strategy, why there always has to be a backup defender behind the first line of defense.

Look now at diagram 78. This shows exactly what should happen when the halfback D5 has been beaten. A2 retains the ball; naturally, he will be opposed by D2, who moves forward to tackle him, thus leaving his space open.

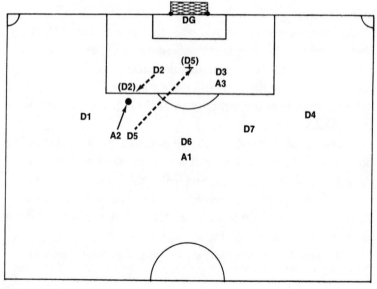

78.

But while that is going on, the beaten halfback D5 races for the penalty spot and fills the gap in the defense.

This interchange of position is an essential of modern soccer; without it the defense can be split wide open by any half-decent attacking line. When the same situation occurs closer to the goal, the beaten man must rush back to the goalpost nearest to him.

Diagram 79 shows what can happen if the beaten defender does not take up his new position. Again D2 moves forward to tackle the attacker A2, only this time the space behind him is open because D5 is standing around idly, hoping his colleague is going to beat the attacker.

Instead, A2 avoids being tackled by passing into the open where attacker A3, rushing forward, can collect the

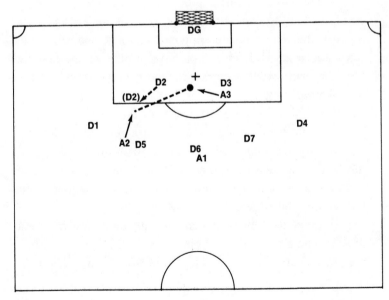

79.

pass, and head across clear, wide-open space to score a goal.

This kind of tactical defense can be practiced in the "freeze" style. First the players walk through the drill. Then, this time with the ball, walk through it again. Once the defense understands the principle, they should practice it in a scrimmage.

Zonal Marking

The principle of zone defense is that players cover imaginary defined areas, instead of one-to-one marking. In essence this means that a defender will only be concerned with an attacker who enters his zone; if the attacker leaves, the defender will relinquish him to the defender covering the adjoining zone.

There are some initial problems in learning this type of defense. Man-to-man marking is easy to understand—you identify the man you are supposed to mark and stick with him. But in zonal defense, you have to play a zone first and then the man. Some players will find it very difficult at first to make the switch.

Naturally, there are differences of opinion as to how the zones should be allocated. One area of agreement is the division of the field into thirds. Diagram 80 shows the defensive third. This is an overlapping system. Zones 1 and 2 each cover an area bounded by the touchlines, an imaginary centerline, and the edge of the defensive third.

A point to remember here: not all fields are the same dimensions, but the marked-out areas on the field are. Thus, the penalty area is always 44 yards wide by 18 yards deep.

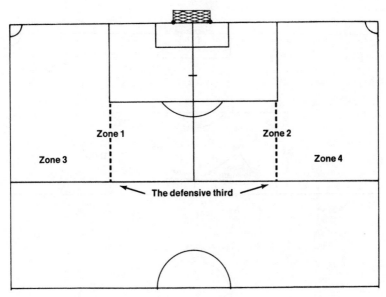

80.

Therefore, the narrow zones on the wings, which are marked from the penalty-area line, will vary in width depending on the size of the field.

In other words, on a small field, say 60 yards across, those corridors will each be only 8 yards wide. On a larger field—80 yards across—they will be 18 yards wide. A secondary consideration—the length of the field can also vary, and thus the depth of the defensive third will change.

In diagram 81 the defenders are set up as in diagram 76, that is, using a backsweeper D2. In this style of defense he is the one zoneless player, being able to cross into either of the zones as he is needed.

D1 and 4 are assigned to cover zone 1, D3 and 6, zone 2,

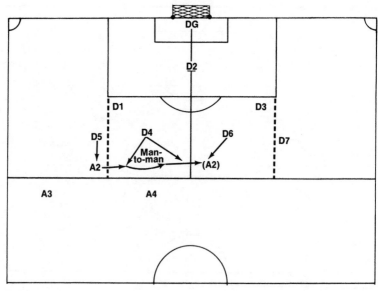

81.

and the outside halfbacks the wing corridors, zones 3 and 4. Also shown in diagram 81 is an example of how an attacker (A2) should be handled. As he travels with the ball across the width of the field, he moves through three zones. In each case he is approached by a defender whom, let us say, he beats or avoids. They do not chase him but relinquish him to the player covering the adjoining zone.

It can be seen how zonal play tends to allow a defense that is under pressure to hold up. In diagram 81, A2 could well have passed off to either A3 or A4, but because the defenders had not moved out of their zone, the attackers would not have gained any penetration.

Of course, a team cannot solve all its defensive problems by adopting a zonal defense. It must still contend with the comparable skills of its opponents. But once its principles have been mastered, the system can often prevent an attacking force from splitting it wide open.

An Attacking Defense

When the halfbacks become an integral part of the defensive lineup, a team may give the impression that it is adopting the kind of game that was once very popular with European teams. The principle then was to use a formation such as 4–4–2 to pack the goal area with defenders and bank on breakaways to score goals. Not surprisingly, the number of goals scored in those games was low—something that didn't please the crowds, who wanted to see an exciting attack game.

But a well-organized defense does not require a team that is only strong in its own half. The key to the balance between defense and attack is the halfback line. It would be unfair to say that any one soccer position is more important than another, but it is true that few outstanding teams could have achieved their greatness without a superb halfback line.

The halfback line is often called "the engine room," because it is from the midfield that the power of the game, either in attack or defense, is most often generated. The halfback, particularly in a fast-moving game, sees more of the ball than most. For instance, if a team is under constant attack, then its forwards do not have much to do. Conversely, if a team is on the attack, then its back line can only play a supporting role. But in either case the halfbacks are involved.

The halfbacks have to be in superb physical condition. A player will not be able to be up with the attackers one minute and back supporting the defense in the next if he is not fit. So it is a good idea for a team to have in their substitute group a preponderance of halfbacks.

To use the halfback line as a necessary part of its defense and be able to switch suddenly into attack, a team must remember that it is not only forwards who score goals. Modern soccer has produced innovations in player position. It is now not at all uncommon for a fullback to score a goal, and very often the winghalfs build up almost as high a goal-scoring record as some forwards.

The secret lies in fluidity. A team must have a philosophy of flexibility, so that the players can educate themselves to take opportunities.

The Goalkeeper as an Attacker

The goalkeeper is looked on as the last line of defense. By that very virtue he is also often the first line of attack. When the goalkeeper has the ball, his team has possession—the name of the game—and he is in a position to initiate the first of a series of attacking plays.

In youth soccer when the goalkeeper has possession of the ball, he has a number of advantages over the other players: the rules do not permit him to be touched or harassed. He may, therefore, move with the ball without fear of being tackled, thus giving him extra time in which to make a decision.

However, in the 1960s FIFA introduced a rule for goalkeepers which was designed to speed up the game (Law XII). This law states that goalkeepers can travel no farther than four steps while they have possession. The way around the rule is for the goalie to roll the ball in front of him, pick it up, go four more steps, then roll it again, and so on. This makes him vulnerable, of course, because an attacker is permitted to attempt to take the ball from the goalie while it is out of his possession and rolling along the ground.

Spectators are always impressed when they see the goalie take a couple of steps and then give the ball a gigantic high boot up the field. What they fail to realize is that the ball often ends up on the head, or at the feet, of an opponent. In other words, the goalie has very spectacularly given the ball away. Except in exceptional circumstances—such as when the opponents crowd the defensive zone and leave their own half clear of players and wide open for a long ball to be collected by a forward—the most productive pass from a goalkeeper is the throw.

Whèn a player makes a foot pass, he momentarily looks up in the direction he wants to put the ball, then his eyes go down as he makes the kick. But when a goalie throws the ball, he need never look at it—he doesn't have to strike it in a particular place, just hold it properly—so he is able to survey the field for a greater length of time and see which players are in the most advantageous positions.

As with kicking, there are various ways of throwing the ball. For a long throw, the goalie should use the four steps he is allowed to gain momentum. His arm should come from behind and he should hurl the ball out into the field of play.

On a short throw along the ground to a close defender,

the arm should be brought down, underarm, and the ball rolled along the ground. For a quick clearance, the action is like shot-putting, the hand well behind the ball with the power coming from the shoulder.

Whichever throw is used, though, the goalie must start out holding the ball in both hands, and only when he goes into his forward movement, release the ball to the throwing hand. Finally, on a wet field the ball is going to become very slippery, so a goalie should wear a pair of good-quality goal-keeping gloves.

The purpose of a goal kick, whether taken by the goal-keeper or a fullback, is to clear the ball upfield and into the possession of one's own teammates. It stands to reason that the longer and higher the kick, the longer it is in the air. This means everyone on the field can watch its flight—including the opponents whose object is to regain possession.

What then are the alternatives? A goal kick can be looked on as a pass or, viewed another way, as an indirect free kick—a placed, dead ball that is to be kicked back into play.

Not every goalkeeper is capable of taking goal kicks. Either his direction is poor or his power is limited. (By *power* is meant the speed at which the ball travels once it has been kicked.) If this is the case, then obviously one or more of the fullbacks must take the kicks.

There is, however, one set-piece goal kick that every goalkeeper should master. Diagram 82 shows the goalkeeper kicking the ball to the edge of the penalty area (the ball must cross the penalty-area line to be in play) to defender D1. The goalie runs toward the line as soon as he has made the kick to

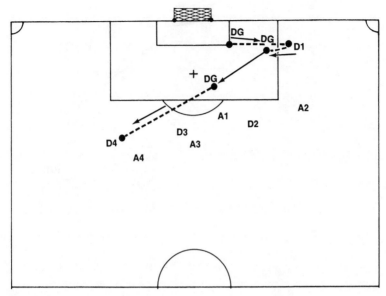

82.

collect the return pass from D1. In the diagram he then moves with the ball, taking his four steps, rolling the ball, four more steps, and so on, until he is ready to make his pass.

Because players are drawn toward the ball and, therefore, the player in possession, the bulk of the attackers will usually be on the side of the field where the kick is being taken. This is why the goalie should "switch" the play by passing across the area to defender D4, on the opposite side of the field. An attack has been initiated.

Goalkeepers often make this kind of pass from a drop kick. Instead of making the kick a volley, the keeper should learn to use the half-volley. Kicking the ball while it is in the

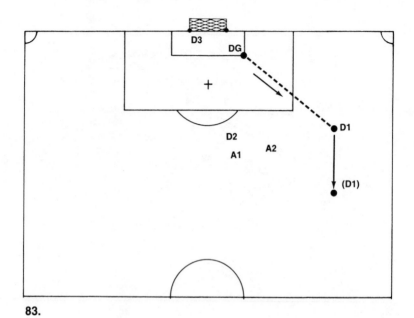

83.

air will almost always produce a high ball and therefore less accuracy. A half-volley, making the kick almost simultaneously as the ball bounces back from the ground, will result in a lower trajectory and greater accuracy.

Until a player taking the goal kicks has attained consistent accuracy, it is preferable that the goal kicks be made to the outside of the field, up along the wings, because most of the opponents are usually congregated in the middle of the field.

This is also why it is often better to use the kick as a common pass, and it need not be a long one. In diagram 83 the goalkeeper is taking the kick. Traditionally, he would try a long one over the heads of A1 and A2 into the middle of the field. Instead, the kick is made as a 20-yard ground pass to defender D1, who is off to the side unmarked, and who can move down the wing with the ball. Note that defender D3 covers the goalmouth while the goalie is taking the kick.

Using the goal kick in this way requires confidence because a defense under pressure is tempted just to get the ball out of the defensive third of the field. But if the players can maintain their composure, they will stand a far better chance of overcoming the attackers and initiating their own attack.

Tactical Attack

The purpose of attack is to confuse the defense, split it open, and press for a goal. An attacking force has to have a mixture of ingredients if it is to be successful: speed, versatility, cunning, and desire are a few of them. While running speed is a great asset, speed off the mark is the most essential. Versatility in attack means being able to read the defense's game and adapt accordingly. Cunning means drawing a defender out of position and taking advantage of it. Desire, of course, means being goal hungry.

Years ago it was the norm for teams to use the wings as a major form of thrust and movement into the defensive areas. This gave way to tighter play in the midfield, with short, concentrated passing. The traditional winger was dispensed with, and with him the movement down to the corner flags and then the cross to the center. But there is now a return to the use of the wing player, which tends to open the game up and take it to the sidelines, creating greater space in which to maneuver.

The advantage of wingers is that they are generally only vulnerable from one side, their inner side, the line being on their outer. As many goals are scored from corner kicks, a player who is capable of reproducing a corner kick on the run should have the opportunity.

This leads to a choice of formation, and to opinion and conjecture. A 4–3–3 formation, if it is to provide wingmen, has to call on the halfback line. A 3–3–4 can spread its four men out across the attacking line. In advanced youth soccer, a 4–3–3 formation appears the most useful and versatile. The formation is well structured to take advantage of its halfback line, aided by fullbacks who can suddenly turn into attackers.

It should be remembered that the first move in an attack comes when the whistle blows to start play: the kickoff. Taking the kickoff provides an advantage—possession—which is why a team that has had a goal scored against it restarts play: they are given the advantage.

It should be noted, incidentally, that the laws say that to start play the ball should be kicked forward into the opponents' half. The kicker may not touch the ball a second time until it has been touched by another player, and the ball is not in play until it has traveled the distance of its own circumference.

Diagram 84 shows a common kickoff play. The center forward passes forward to his inside left, A3, who in turn puts the ball back to the center half, A5. He then passes forward into the space ahead of the right half, A4. An attack is underway.

One danger here is that the opposing team probably uses the same tactic itself, and one of its inside forwards takes im-

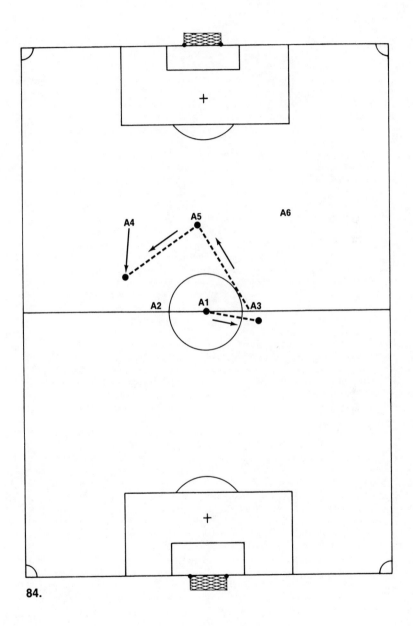

84.

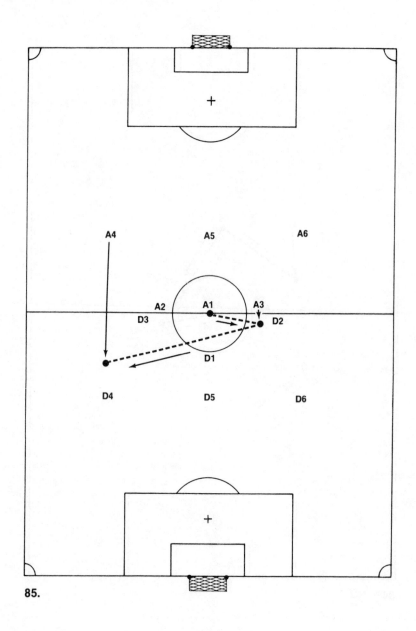

85.

mediate retaliatory action. As soon as the kick is made, an inside forward rushes toward the center half in the hope of beating him to the ball. Very often he makes it and breaks up the play.

It follows that kickoff passes have to be taken swiftly and with precision.

An alternate tactic is shown in diagram 85. Here the center forward again passes to his inside left. This time, though, A3 puts the ball between the space in front of the defending center forward to where his halfback, A4, can collect and press forward.

The Scissors and the Switch

Although experienced players will have overcome the temptation to chase the ball, there will always be a tendency to follow the flow and path of play. This means that if the play is over on the left wing, the attention of the defenders will be focused in that direction.

A thinking attack force can capitalize on this by "drawing" the defense and using open space, just as a magician distracts the audience's attention with his moving hand while his other, concealed hand gets on with the trick. In soccer the moving hand is replaced by a player who has control of the ball; the concealed hand is the player moving into open space.

In diagram 86 the outside right position is played by A1, who moves into the center with the ball. Notice how the defenders will move with him. Meanwhile, the right half, A2, crosses into the open space up the wing. Having "drawn"

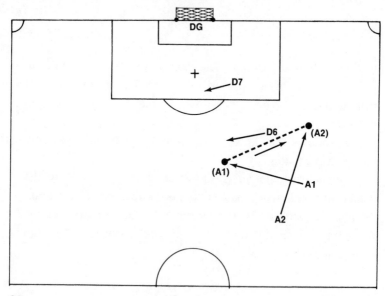

86.

the defense, A1 spins and puts a pass back up the wing to the waiting A2.

A variation known as the scissors move is shown in diagram 87. This time A1 either runs over the ball leaving it for A2 to collect on his way toward the wing, or he can back-heel it to him. The practice and use of the scissors move will demonstrate to players how they can fool a defense and create space for themselves to maneuver in.

The same idea is behind the switch, meaning switching the play from one side of the field to the other. In diagram 88 the player in the right-half position, A1, cuts across the field toward the opposite side. Naturally, he draws the defense, leaving the right wing more or less open. When A1 reaches the far side of the penalty area, he "switches" the play by making a long pass back to the right side to the waiting wing-man, A2.

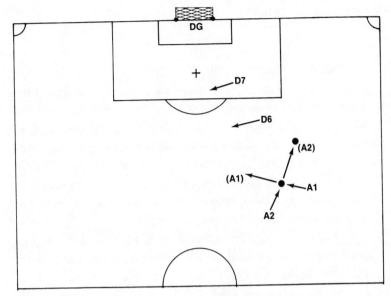

87.

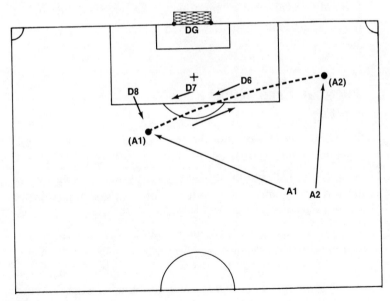

88.

Modern soccer, with its emphasis on fluidity, has brought new terms, particularly for the forward line. Forwards are now often called "strikers" or "front runners." In these two small sections on the scissors and the switch play, A1 is called "the player in the outside right position," not the outside right. The reason for this is because forward players no longer consistently stick to one fixed position but interchange not only between themselves but between the halfbacks and sometimes even the fullbacks.

Today a successful soccer team must be capable of constant movement, versatility, and alertness. Years ago when a player wore the number 11 shirt, everyone knew he was the left-winger. They expected him to be on the left wing at all times. Not anymore. He may start out playing there, and will certainly spend most of his time in the left-hand side of the field, but he is no longer restricted to that specifically defined area.

Tactical Free Kicks

More than any other soccer-playing nation, Brazil taught the world how devastating the free kick could be. They were strongly aided, of course, by Pelé and Rivelino. Pelé has been accused of setting up free kicks by deliberately hitting the turf and going into a little act of pain and injury in an effort to persuade the referee that he has been fouled. As he was, in fact, often genuinely fouled, it is not surprising that on a few occasions the ploy worked. Pelé, of course, wasn't the only player to pull that piece of deception. What this shows is the importance given to the advantage of being awarded a free kick.

Direct free kicks, naturally, require no group tactical finesse. What they do require is a kicker who has a shot like a cannon, and preferably one who can put a good curve on the ball. The West German, Zimmermann, is one of the finest exponents of the direct free kick in today's soccer. The interesting thing about Zimmermann is that he is a fullback, which demonstrates nicely the point that the most proficient kicker is not necessarily a forward.

Indirect free kicks, however, require tactical plays. They also provide a dramatic setting, because, apart from the corner kick, they are the only soccer situations that allow a preliminary setup where the players, on both sides, jostle and act out what often looks like stage directions. That is exactly what they are doing.

The position on the field from which the free kick is to be taken dictates to a certain extent the alignment of the defense. The attacking players making the kick have the advantage because they are originating the strategy—the defense can only try to determine it.

Direct kicks taken within goal-scoring range almost always call for the defense to make a "wall." The position of the wall and the number of players in it will depend upon the angle of the kick.

As far as the defense is concerned, the goalkeeper is in absolute charge here. Experienced goalkeepers, who are aware of their own capabilities and limitations, will set the wall to suit their particular abilities.

Generally, if the kick is coming from the center, the wall should have four players and should cover the area from one goalpost inward, the goalkeeper thus having plenty of room to see the ball and the kicker. If the angle is more acute, fewer players can be used in the wall, and it should then cover the space from the nearest goalpost inward.

The attackers will try to outfox the defense. The most successful indirect free kicks are the ones that are the simplest and involve the minimum number of players: two. Using complicated plays and more than two players to accomplish them leaves a team open to error.

The Laws of the Game say that on an indirect free kick a goal cannot be scored unless the ball has been played or touched by a player other than the kicker before passing through the goal. At the same time the opposing players shall be at least 10 yards from the ball while the kick is being taken.

It is this rule which has created the traditional method of taking the kick. Because the opposition is at least 10 yards away, there is time for a short pass to be made, without fear of interception, to a second kicker who will then put a shot in on goal.

Obviously, the attackers will try somehow to set themselves up so that they can beat the wall, then the goalkeeper. The initial kicker needs no particularly specialized skill other than to feint a kick in one direction and pass the ball accurately to the second kicker, who will make the shot. He must have the ability to curve the ball, make it dip from a long shot, and all this with tremendous power.

There are rarely more than a couple of times during a game when potentially goal-scoring indirects are awarded, so there is little reason for a team to assemble a lengthy portfolio of tactical plays. A few good maneuvers, based on the examples to be given, should do very well. The kick-taking

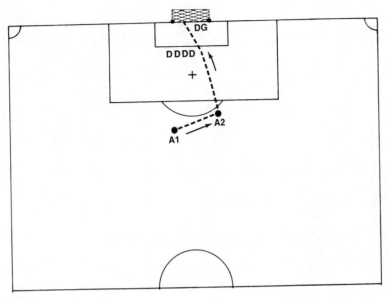

89.

players have to be thoroughly rehearsed, confident, and capable of taking advantage of the infringement.

Diagram 89 shows the classic play. A four-man wall has been set up to cover the space from the left post to the center of the goal. The keeper stands ready, near the far post, giving him an uninterrupted view of the kicker. The initial kicker, A1, passes to A2, who powers a shot between the outside of the wall and the goalkeeper. Note that the shot has a curve to it.

Diagram 90 shows a variation. There is nothing in the laws that says an attacker may not join the defensive wall. Here we see that attacker, A3, has joined the wall on the middle goal side. Again the classic pass is made from A1 to

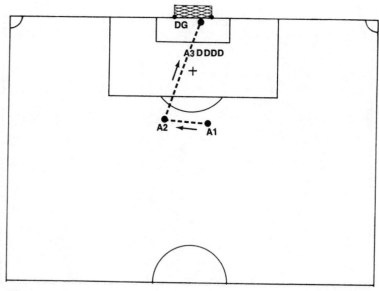

90.

A2, but this time the kicker aims at the wall, or more specifically, at his own man, A3. Naturally, A3, who knows what the play is all about and doesn't want to be hit, very speedily ducks out of the way. Because he has obscured the goalkeeper's view, the ball passes over him and into the goal.

When the attacking line sets up this kind of play, it would obviously be wise for the defense to place a player behind A3 to block the through ball.

Diagram 91 illustrates how a long, dipping kick should be made. Because of the way the attackers have positioned themselves, there is no chance of slipping a curve shot around the wall. This time A2 has to place a shot over the

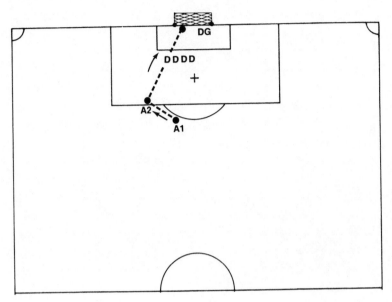

91.

heads of the wall, which will either dip toward the ground or power itself into the upper corner of the net.

There is a lot of fun to be had working out the various indirect free-kick plays. However, as in all soccer tactics, the move has to be well practiced in advance and kept as simple as possible.

THE PRACTICAL SIDE OF SOCCER

Equipment

A soccer player's equipment list is, fortunately, short. The uniform—shirt, shorts, and socks—is usually supplied by a player's club, and the cost is generally included in the seasonal fee paid to the club. Some youth clubs provide matching sweat suits and carryalls, but if they do not, it is advisable for a player to have his own sweat suit and a bag in which to carry his soccer shoes.

The use of a sweat suit will, of course, depend on the climate in which the player lives—but even in sunny California it gets cold in the winter, and a cold player is one prone to injury. Since soccer shoes should only be worn on the field—wearing them on the sidewalk will not only damage the cleats but could result in an ankle injury—it is easier if the player has something in which to carry them.

Some players like to wear shin guards, and it is a good idea for young players to get used to them. They will protect the front of the lower leg and take the sting out of a blow. There are a number of styles available, from cheap plastic ones to the type that is built into an oversock. Whichever style is used, the important thing is that they do not have sharp, stiff edges. Goalkeepers often use knee and elbow pads to protect themselves, particularly from the results of a dive across the goal.

Soccer balls are usually supplied by the club. There are more than two hundred brands of soccer balls available in the United States. While the choice may depend on the money available, different balls behave differently in different climates. If you live in a consistently hot or cold climate, it is wise to check with your local professional team or soccer supplier for the right ball.

Generally speaking, the sensible thing to do is to buy a cheap, molded rubber ball, if it will be used in the street or on a hardtop playing area. An expensive leather ball would be damaged in these circumstances. The inexpensive ball costs about $10.

Practice balls for use on the field should be waterproof, or they will become soggy and heavy and difficult to kick when wet. They should also closely approximate the style and weight of the ball to be used in the actual game. If players practice kicking with one style of ball and then switch to a different type for their game, it can upset their timing.

The major manufacturers usually make a fine-quality game ball and a less expensive practice ball. Prices range from about $25 for a good-quality practice ball to $60 for a top-quality game ball.

The major item on any soccer player's equipment list is his soccer shoes. There are approximately thirty companies manufacturing and distributing soccer shoes. Shoes vary from cheap plastic ones to sophisticated, top-quality leather designs.

Prices range from $15 to $60. Most manufacturers produce excellent shoes in the middle-price range. Before a young player purchases soccer shoes, he should keep in mind that they will only last one season, not only because he will have outgrown them, but because even the best shoes can only withstand a season's wear and tear.

Soccer Shoes and Players' Feet

It is imperative that soccer shoes fit properly. The wrong pair of shoes can eventually ruin a young person's feet. If there is any doubt about fit, consult a foot specialist. The following explanation about the structure of the foot and choosing the right kind of shoe comes from Dr. Joseph R. Bartis, a distinguished podiatrist from Oakland, California.

Man's foot is an engineering work of art. The foot is an organ in the best sense of the word, although we generally think of internal organs first. It is a highly specialized organ of weight bearing, which enables us to perform a function of great importance—locomotion—movement from place to place.

There are approximately twenty-six bones in each foot; numerous ligaments, which bind bone to bone and stabilize the structures; and there are four layers of muscles on the undersurface of the foot, as well as several muscles on the dorsum, or top, of the foot. All of the muscles of the lower leg (below the knee) have tendons that attach to the structures of the foot.

Purchasing a pair of soccer shoes can be a difficult and

confusing experience, since there are so many varieties available. For the beginning soccer player, *fit* is the prime concern, rather than style or popular brand name or even color. Growing feet cannot be restricted by faulty-fitting shoes because deformities can occur in these generally flexible, moldable-type feet.

Fit involves several factors which are critical:

1. Heel-to-ball ratio
2. Toe room

The individual should always be in a weight-bearing (standing) position while being measured for soccer boots or shoes. Sitting while being measured does not allow for the normal expansion of the foot and can result in a false measurement, both in length and width. Heel-to-ball ratio is a measurement of the distance from the back portion of the heel to the ball of the foot (the area which is designated as the first metatarsal head). This is located at the base of the great toe (see diagram 92A).

If this relationship is not correct, the foot may either receive abnormal pressure on the great toe joint and/or the foot will tend to slide or slip back and forth in the shoe. Toe room is equally as important for growing feet. We must not restrict normal growth patterns by too short a shoe. As a rule of thumb, the shoe should be about one-half inch longer than the ends of the toes. In younger children, where a more rapid rate of growth may be expected, one may obtain the shoe a little longer than one-half inch to allow for growth, but great care must be taken so that it does not slip off the foot (see diagram 92B).

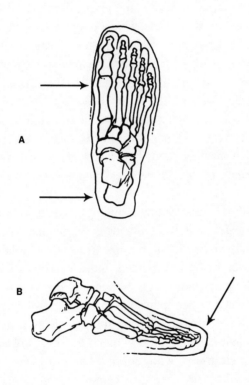

92. A. Heel-to-ball ratio. B. Correct shoe size.

Materials also vary. The youth-soccer player should look for a shoe constructed of a material which is comfortable with good foot function, that is, plastics or other man-made materials do not allow for circulation of air around the foot; they may be too stiff and may not allow moisture to be evaporated very quickly. Some plastics tend to be brittle and may crack, causing areas which may irritate the skin over bony joint prominences such as the toes, instep, heel, or even ankle joint. Of all the synthetics, nylon, or a combination of nylon and plastic, might be acceptable if cost is a factor.

The best material for shoes is leather. Just as with conventional shoes, leather appears to be the all-around best for prolonged wear and comfort. Some soccer shoes are constructed of leather and nylon combinations—the leather usually being placed at the stress points of the shoe: toe and heel.

Another consideration in buying a soccer shoe is the sole and its cleats. The most practical is the one-piece molded sole, usually made of high-impact plastic materials: that is, the cleats and sole are molded into a one-piece unit. Cleats may wear down with usage, but usually the shoe will also be worn and need to be replaced at that time, also. The length of the cleat should not be too long so as to create instability and to create a situation where too much traction is obtained and, therefore, interferes with normal running. This can occur when long cleats are used on a hard or frozen surface. Longer cleats should generally be used on muddy or softer, grassy fields.

Removable cleats or "screw-ins" are not really necessary for the average beginning player. The cleat length should not exceed one and one-half inches. Regarding the proper fit of shoes, it is imperative to obtain a last of proper shape to prevent pinching of the toes. The toe-box area should be rounded, and not pointed, as in some poorly made shoes.

Lastly, the longitudinal arch of the shoe should be supportive yet supple enough to allow for flexion and extension. Too flexible an arch will create foot fatigue and muscle imbalance, as well as joint strain. Too firm an arch will not allow the foot to flex and extend normally and will restrict normal motion.

Injuries

Soccer injuries, particularly in the younger age groups, tend not to be too severe. Most center around the feet and legs, although two players colliding when they both try for a high ball can result in a pair of sore heads.

The ideal situation for any team, of course, is to have a parent who is a doctor—better still, one who is a member of the American Orthopaedic Society for Sports Medicine.

In any event, it would be wise for a club or district to establish contact with such a member, as not all doctors are well informed about athletic injuries. Sports medicine is a specialization on its own; names and addresses of members can be obtained by writing to:

American Orthopaedic Society for Sports Medicine
430 North Michigan Avenue
Chicago, Ill. 60611

If a team is without a doctor, at least one person should be asked to be responsible for a first-aid kit. It would help if that person also had some qualified knowledge of first aid. First-aid kits can be bought or assembled. In addition to the usual kit contents, it is advisable to carry a supply of six-inch-wide elastic bandages and some inexpensive cardboard splints.

It is mandatory that a supply of ice is taken to every game. There are also a number of ice packs available, either disposable or reusable, and at least one of these should be carried.

It is essential that an ample supply of liquids is available at every game. This is even more important in warm or hot climates. When the body becomes overheated, it loses body salt and fluids that must be replaced. If they are not, players will complain about leg cramps and the like. However, salt tablets should *never* be given.

Under no circumstances should carbonated drinks be given to players at halftime. A great many doctors recommend Gatorade as the best halftime drink. Although it tends to be expensive when bought by the bottle, it is also available in powder form.

The most common injuries that occur during a soccer game involve the feet and lower extremities. Dr. Joseph R. Bartis describes and discusses them below.

STRAINS AND SPRAINS

These injuries occur when a joint or joints are stretched or twisted past their normal ability to move (range of motion). The usual areas sprained are the medial and lateral areas of the ankle joints, just below the ankle bones. The base of the great toe may be sprained due to direct pressure from the end of the toe after kicking a ball or other firm object. These sprains and strains result from either stretching a ligament or muscle to actual tears of these structures, complete or incomplete. Incomplete tears or stretching of the structures may result in swelling, pain, and limitation of movement. Complete tears may result in instability of the joint or severe pain along the course of a muscle. Severe swelling may also occur.

Sprains and strains should not be taken lightly, as they can possibly lead to pain and deformity in later years, as well as chronic instability of a joint.

The treatment of these conditions is directed toward immediate application of ice packs to the area followed by immobilization of the part, usually with an elastic bandage to keep the part from moving excessively, thereby allowing the part to heal. Adhesive strapping is frequently utilized to support the affected joint or tendon or muscle. These strappings are applied at weekly intervals for three or four weeks. This may take anywhere from two to three weeks to six weeks in more complicated situations. Plastic casting may be necessary in some cases so that complete immobilization can be accomplished.

DISLOCATIONS

These are the disruption of joints, so that the joint surfaces may slip past each other, and the joint loses its normal shape or contour. Dislocations may be partial or complete. The toes are relatively easy to dislocate, and these problems require medical attention to reduce the deformity. Do not attempt to forcefully manipulate any joint. Immobilize the part and transport the patient to a medical facility.

FRACTURES OF THE FOOT

Fractures of the bones of the feet and ankles are not very common during the play of soccer. These fractures are generally associated with the toes and metatarsal bones, although ankle and leg fractures are not rare. The causes of fractures may either be direct injury or indirect. Indirect injury can be caused by stress on the bone, as opposed to a direct hit on the bone. The immediate evidence of a fracture is swelling, discoloration, pain, and difficulty in movement of the part. Fractures also may be closed or open. Open fractures are those in which the bone protrudes from the surface of the skin.

The principles of first aid apply, that is, immediate inspection and treatment of a possible fracture. (It is not always simple to decide whether a bone is fractured, so if there is any doubt, one should treat the injury as a fracture.) This is done by splinting or immobilizing the part. Toe fractures usually require three to four weeks for healing, and there is generally no disability afterward. Activity can be resumed after that time. The great toe is the most important toe and should be given the most attention, since deformities may result in permanent disabilities. Fractures of the metatarsal bones (instep area) require four to six weeks of immobilization. After that, two to three weeks are needed before full activity may be resumed. Ankles are the most frequently injured joints in sports, especially soccer. Swelling. pain, discoloration, and limitation of motion are the signs of ankle fracture. Immediate application of ice, followed by splinting of the ankle, is necessary. No walking or standing is permitted on the extremity. The injured player should be transported to a hospital for X rays and treatment as soon as possible. Delay in treatment could result in complications which might well prolong healing.

Fatigue fractures, or stress fractures, can occur in the metatarsal bones, ankle bones, and lower leg bones. They may not show up for two to three weeks after injury and can mimic sprains and may be missed on first examination. If pain or disability persists, one should X-ray the part again after two weeks.

Contusions are injuries which are caused by a direct blow to the foot, or more likely the shins. They may be quite painful but usually are not disabling and may be handled very adequately by direct application of ice packs, followed by padding of the area with felt or lamb's wool. Shin pads in younger players will help to prevent these injuries. Later on, heat and massage may be helpful if painful symptoms persist.

HEEL CONDITIONS

A common problem for players ages 10 to 14 is the condition called "epiphysitis," which occurs at the back part of the heel where the Achilles tendon attaches to the bone. This usually results in tenderness and pain when the shoe rubs on the heel or during running. At times this can be so severe that limping is evident. Treatment for this condition is based on padding of the heel of the shoe with felt and application of moist heat to the area. A cessation of running for ten to fourteen days may be necessary. And, in some cases, plaster casting for four weeks may be used in chronically painful conditions.

SUMMARY

Foot problems should not be taken too lightly. Many injuries which have occurred early in life, and been mistreated, or not treated at all, may become chronic disabilities later on. This may prevent a child from actively pursuing athletics. Remember, feet are organs in the true sense of the word (organs of weight bearing) and should be afforded the same respect as any other part of our anatomy.

ICE OR HEAT?

The question often arises whether ice or heat should be used on an injury. Dr. James P. Nevins of Berkeley, California, who is a specialist in sports medicine, offers the following advice.

Any traumatic injury where there is internal bleeding (by this is meant minute bleeding which is not always discernible to the naked eye), sprained shoulder, sprained knee, torn muscle, or any similar injury, should initially be controlled by ice. The sooner the better.

The ice causes a constriction of the blood vessels, thereby reducing the amount of blood flow. The more blood that collects in the injured area, the longer it will take to heal.

Do not apply ice directly to the skin; either use an ice pack—which has a protective coating—or wrap the ice in an

Ace bandage or cloth. Be certain the wrapping is not too tight, or the blood supply may be cut off. Leave the ice on the area for about half an hour, then take it off for about fifteen minutes. Then repeat the procedure.

Ice is generally used for the first three days, then heat is applied. The reason for this is that for the first three days an effort is made to cut down the bleeding, to allow as little as possible. However, there will be a small blood clot of some kind, thus causing pain; the larger the clot, the greater the pain. The heat is used to try and dissolve the clot and so reduce the pain.

Rest and, if necessary, elevation of the injured area are essential. Resumption of activity should not be made until all the swelling and discomfort have totally disappeared.

If in any doubt at all, consult your doctor.

The rule for any injury that is obviously causing pain is caution. If it appears that a bone has been broken, the limb should be immobilized and a splint applied. The person should then either be taken to the nearest hospital or an ambulance should be called.

NAMATH KNEE

When any young athlete complains about soreness or pain in the knee, football player Joe Namath and his injured knees come to mind. It is unlikely that a young soccer player is suffering from the same complaint. More likely, he is going through a phase in his physical development which will pass with age. As youngsters reach puberty, their bones are growing faster than their muscles and/or tendons. Very little can be done about it except treating it with a little heat and resting it. However, If the pain becomes acute, consult your doctor.

Diet

There are many myths about an athlete's diet, but all authorities agree that steak and eggs is not a good meal for an athlete. Steak is a poor source of immediate energy, since it takes too long to digest and can actually be a hindrance to athletic performance.

The best foods for athletic performance are those high in carbohydrates, particularly potatoes, pasta, and bread. An ideal before-game breakfast is cereal, low-fat milk, some toast or even pancakes, and natural fruit juice. If a child already has a weight problem, then a dietician or his doctor should be consulted. The chances are that an overweight youth will not go very far in soccer.

PLAYING THE GAME

Warming Up

Most youth-soccer clubs require all players to provide certificates of good health from their family doctors. But even a young player in good physical condition should not walk out onto a soccer field and start playing without first warming up.

Warm-up exercises should not be confused with the exercises done in a training program. In the first instance, a player is preparing himself for strenuous activity to follow; in the second, he is conditioning himself.

Failure to warm up before a soccer game, or any other vigorous activity for that matter, is asking for trouble. The trouble will most probably be a strained or torn muscle fiber.

Performance will improve if the muscles are *slightly* warmed up before a game. There is some controversy, even in professional circles, about the value of excessive warm-ups. Many professional athletes and coaches disdain the calisthenic approach.

It is best to warm up gradually. Starting off with a few violent jumping jacks or grasspeckers is a good example of what *not* to do. It is far better to begin with a little light jogging in place, followed by leg-stretching exercises.

A player who warms up too soon before a game, say 20 minutes or more, and then stands around waiting or even resting has a good chance of stiffening up and being in worse condition than when he started. Also, if a player begins to sweat, he is dissipating energy needed for the game.

Coaches should keep this in mind when substituting players. The replacement player, who has been sitting on the sidelines waiting for his chance to play, will have become cold and stiff—the worst possible physical condition. Therefore, coaches should plan ahead. A few minutes before a substitution is intended, the replacement player should start to warm up, as is done in professional games.

A secondary purpose of a warm-up is to prepare the muscles and joints that will be called on to function most during the game. Obviously, in soccer a player is not going to use his biceps, so there is not much point in doing arm exercises. (The exception is goalkeepers, who should do a few simple and gentle arm-stretching exercises.)

One of the best preliminary exercises after the general warm-up is for the team to form a large circle, with one or two men in the center. Players forming the circle pass the ball across it; the players in the middle try to intercept. When the ball is intercepted, the last kicker replaces the player in the middle. Apart from being fun to do, this accomplishes two things: it prepares the leg muscles for the job they will have to do on the field, and it reinforces an important soccer function—passing.

Warm-ups are generally done on the sidelines. Practice

should take place on the field. For practice, the team should split up—the forwards and the goalkeeper going into the penalty area for shooting practice, and the halfbacks and backs into the remainder of their half of the field for further passing practice.

Players should not overdo pregame practice. Goalies can injure themselves in a pregame practice by being overenthusiastic.

The Inner Game

The inner game of soccer is nothing new, although interest in the subject is now more widespread. A number of serious studies have been made into the relationship between the attainment of a physical skill and the part mental involvement plays in its development and improvement.

Sports and games where a single player pits himself against a single opponent (tennis being one example; billiards and chess even better ones) obviously present an entirely different set of difficulties than collective sports, but all of them have a common problem—competition and its concomitant stress.

Team sports create additional challenges. The soccer environment, where twenty-two players are in constant movement (twenty, actually, not counting the goalkeepers) and where instant decisions have to be made, presents the individual player with an array of problems.

Skill, in itself, can become secondary to performance, the one not necessarily being totally dependent upon the other. How many players shine in practice sessions only to disappoint the coach and themselves in a competitive game?

Why do players whose skills have been admirably demonstrated go off form? How do athletes come back?

Players will try hard to overcome whatever is stopping them from making the best use of their abilities, but more often than not, the harder they try, the worse it gets.

To complicate matters, in soccer a coach is dealing not only with the problems of his players, but with the collective personality of the team. This problem may not arise with an Under-8 team, but in the older age groups and in the professional teams, where the basic skills have been learned, a player will be more concerned with his performance abilities, and will have to learn more sophisticated techniques.

There is a mental time lag between learning a new skill and understanding and becoming proficient at it. This period of mental ''catching up'' will vary with individual players. Some will grasp a new technique very quickly, others will need more time. This is particularly so in team tactics where all eleven members of the team have to learn how to work together.

This problem becomes apparent when the relative abilities of our national teams are compared with their European counterparts. The individual skills—ball control, dribbling, and so on—seem comparable. The gap lies in the group performance of these skills and the team's understanding of what should be going on—how the pace and flow of the game are controlled. What compounds the problem is that of growing up in a country that has only recently embraced soccer. Children in other countries have grown up absorbing it.

Many great athletes will tell you that once the mechanics

of a skill have been thoroughly learned, there comes a point where, somehow, the unconscious takes over. It has been said of Pelé that he could "see" the entire field in a soccer game, just "know" where the other players were and what they would be doing next.

Players cannot reach that stage without work, and Pelé certainly did that, hour after hour, day after day. His genius did not suddenly happen overnight—it was a long, hard struggle.

There is some evidence that during sleep the mind can be put to use to improve one's abilities. Many soccer players have reported that they have learned to rehearse in their sleep, "practicing" a certain stroke or move. Even without going out onto the field and practicing, a player has improved, for instance, the way he takes a corner kick by letting his mind go over the technique in his sleep.

Visualization also appears to have great value. The very fact of visualizing oneself doing better seems very often to produce an improvement. Visualization on its own is not a method of suddenly improving one's game. It must be combined with actual physical practice, and it is the combination of the two that seems to be so effective. The ability to perform this kind of improvement technique will vary between players; some appear to do it without quite realizing what is happening. Very often it is this kind of player who inspires a team.

Teams develop reputations for being able to come back in a game where they are trailing. Sometimes it is the coach who is able to "fire them up," and other times it is just one player who is somehow able to instill in his teammates the will to win, to accomplish what may seem to be impossible.

The making of the inner player is not easy to describe. There is no prescribed set of exercises which will suit or work for everyone. One simple example which a soccer player might try is to take a penalty kick. This is a stress-making situation—perhaps the outcome of the game will depend on the result, and the responsibility can be immense. In theory, the kick is simple to do and the outcome should always be assured, because properly placed, there is no goalkeeper on earth who can save a hard, low shot that goes just inside one of the uprights. The kick is taken from only 12 yards out, and the goalie may not move until the kick is made. However, as we all know, and some have experienced, it does not always work that way. Penalty kicks are missed, or the ball is shot straight at the goalkeeper for an easy save.

For the practical part of this exercise the use of a soccer backboard is a great help. If there isn't one available, the player should place a target in the goal at which to aim.

The night before practice, when you go to bed, try the following: lie flat on your back and gently tense all the muscles of the body and then relax them. Beginning with the toes, relax all the muscles in your body, mentally telling them to relax. Breathe in deeply from the diaphragm through the nose. As the air comes in, you will feel your stomach rise. Visualize the air coming into your lungs—do not strain or raise your shoulders. Hold the breath for a few seconds and then slowly breathe out through the nose. Again visualize the air leaving your lungs, then suck in your diaphragm until all the air has been expended. Slowly repeat the exercise. It will be very pleasant, and at first you may drift off into a quiet sleep.

Once you have developed this routine, you will find that you do not immediately go to sleep. As you lie in bed, slowly breathing properly, picture in your mind the goal, either as it is drawn on the backboard or an actual goal. See the soccer ball standing on the penalty spot.

You are going to take the kick and put the ball in the right-hand side of the goal, just inside the upright and about 3 feet off the ground. In slow motion, mentally make the kick; watch the ball slowly sail through the air toward your target; see it hit the target.

Go through the kick time and time again. Increase the speed of the ball until it goes into the goal like a shot out of a cannon. Enjoy the feeling of pleasure you will get as the ball ends up in the back of the net. Then drift off into a pleasant sleep.

The next day when you are out on the field, practice the kick and do it exactly as you visualized yourself doing it the night before. But as you approach the ball, see it in your mind's eye in the back of the net. Then see its flight. Then see it on the penalty spot—in other words, reverse the procedure.

Now take the kick.

If you practice this technique consistently, when you are actually faced with taking a penalty kick, you will find that you do not hear the sounds of the crowd or your teammates—there will be nothing to distract you, and you will score.

Once you have proved to yourself that the method works, try it in combination with a teammate. For example, if you play right half, practice the wall pass with the center half. You both know how to make the pass correctly, but it rarely comes off properly in a game.

First, go through the exact pass on the field, using cones as the opposing players. When you both have a fix on how you want to accomplish the pass, agree to practice it in your minds. If both of you are conscientious, you will find that the next time you make the pass in a game, you both will have improved, and the pass will come off.

Do not think this is a magical method of suddenly becoming a star player, since it may not work with everyone. There is, however, evidence to show that the technique has great value.

On the field of play, total concentration is very important—concentration that blocks out the yells from the spectators, or how cold or hot it is. You should totally immerse yourself so that both your mind and body are working. An athlete, in any sport, is subject to highs and lows, losses and wins, personal problems, his own imagination, his senses and intellect. All these can combine to change the way he functions. A player has to learn to allow his inner self to work for him.

Youth Modifications of the Laws

Most states have their own Youth Soccer Association that is an affiliated branch of and complies with the authority of the United States Youth Soccer Association and the United States Soccer Federation. In northern California, for instance, there is the CYSA—the California Youth Soccer Association.

These organizations are vital to the proper regulation of youth soccer. The officers of the associations are mainly volunteers who devote many hours to the good of the game.

While youth soccer is played by the "Laws of the Game" as published by FIFA, the ultimate authority worldwide, modifications have been made to take into account the age and amateur status of the players. The "Rules of Play" were drawn up, and from time to time amended, by the youth associations.

For example, under the laws the goalkeeper may be charged fairly in his own area, if he has possession of the ball. However, in youth soccer the rules firmly state that charging the goalkeeper shall not be permitted at any time when he/she is within his/her own penalty area.

A coach, players, and even spectators, therefore, should be well informed about not only the Laws of the Game but also the Rules of Play, as laid down by the governing association in their specific geographical area.

Other rules applying to youth soccer are as follows. Coaching from the sidelines—giving direction to one's own team on the points of strategy and position—is permitted provided:

    a. No mechanical devices are used.
    b. The tone of voice is informative and not a harangue.
    c. No coach, substitute, or player is to be anywhere but at his/her bench area during a game.
    d. No coach, substitute, or player is to make derogatory remarks or gestures to the referees, other players, substitutes, or spectators.

   e. No coach, substitute, or player is to use profanity.
   f. No coach, substitute, or player is to incite, in any
      manner, disruptive behavior of any kind.

The penalty for violation of the above rules shall be ejection from the game and disciplinary action.

Most of the rules are commonsense ones designed to control not only the players but also the spectators. (In professional soccer outside the United States, there are steel-mesh fences and guard dogs to do the same thing.)

Differing from professional soccer, the system of substitution in youth soccer has modifications. The number of substitutions in a youth game is unlimited. Professional games generally have a limit of two players. Substitutions may be made as follows:

   a. Prior to a throw-in in your favor.
   b. Prior to a goal kick.
   c. After a goal by either team.
   d. After an injury, be it either team, when the referee
      stops play.
   e. At halftime.
   f. When a player is cautioned, the coach may substitute
      for the cautioned player only.

A substitute player may not enter the field of play until he has been given permission to do so by the referee. The game will start up only after the substituted player has left the field.

A note about rule "f". If a player has been cautioned, that is, given the yellow card and had his name taken by the referee, it is because he has, in the referee's opinion, committed some kind of premeditated foul. If he repeats the action after having been given a caution, then he will be shown the red card and ejected from the game.

A wise coach may feel it is in the best interest of the player, or more so his team, if he is taken off the field to cool down before he goes on to make matters worse; hence the rule.

If a player is shown the red card and ejected, then the team has to continue playing for the duration of the game with ten men only.

The Laws

The USSF in agreement with FIFA publishes a small handbook containing the Laws of the Game. If you want a copy, send $1.50 to:

United States Soccer Federation, Inc.
350 Fifth Avenue
New York, New York 10001

Although there are only seventeen laws, much of the highly detailed directives in them are of little interest to the average youth-soccer player or fan. For instance, it is not vital to know that the lines marking out the parameters of the field should be not more than 5 inches wide.

Here, then, is a summary of the laws for players. While not all the subtleties are covered, all authorized referees are obliged to carry a copy of the official rules with them when they referee a game. It bears repeating that many calls are judgment calls; referees do make mistakes, but not nearly as many as the players and spectators like to make out.

THE BALL IN AND OUT OF PLAY

The ball goes out of play when it completely crosses the goal line or any of the touchlines. The important point to note here is the *whole* of the ball—not part of it.

If the ball rebounds off a goalpost, corner flag, or even the referee, it remains in play provided, of course, it does not rebound over either goal lines or touchlines.

OFFSIDE

The offside call causes more dissension, anger, and frustration than almost any rule in any sport.

To quote the rule book, which in itself can be confusing even to the initiated:

> A player is declared offside if he is nearer his opponent's goal line than the ball at the moment the ball is played. A player cannot be ruled offside if he is in his own half of the field, or when there are two opponents nearer the goal line than he is, or in a case where the ball last touched an opponent or was played by him. There are no offsides on a corner kick, goal kick, or throw-in, or when the ball is dropped by the referee.

(When they say the ball is dropped by the referee, they don't mean he is being clumsy. They mean the ref dropped

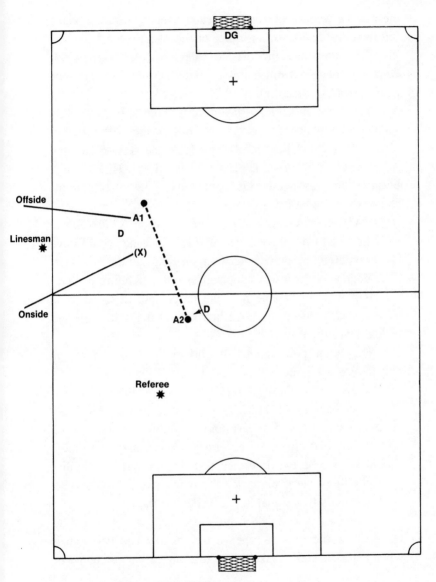

93. The offside rule in diagram.

the ball between a player from each team to restart a game following a holdup for an injury or the like.)

To understand the offside rule, look at diagram 93. Only two players from teams A and D are shown, plus the goalkeeper from team D.

Team A is attacking. Player A2 is about to be tackled by a defending player D, and so he passes the ball forward, across the halfway line, to player A1. At the very instant that A2 *kicks* the ball forward, player A1 is offside. He is offside because he was nearer his opponents' goal line than the ball—when the ball was played.

Had player A1 been in position (x) when A2 *kicked* the ball, he would not have been offside, since he would have had two defending players between himself and the goal line. (The goalkeeper is always counted as one defending player.)

If player A1 had been in the proper position, he could have rushed forward after A2 had kicked the ball, collected it, and headed for goal.

The main point about the offside rule is where the players are when the ball is kicked.

A word in defense of referees. Look at the position of the ref in diagram 93. He is nowhere near where he can accurately make a call. It is just not possible for any ref to keep up with the ball all the time, which is one reason why there should always be two linesmen to help him out. In the diagram the linesman is alongside the play, and he would wave his linesman's flag signaling "offside" to the referee.

There are a couple of situations that are often not as clear-cut as the obvious open-field offside. The first one is when a corner kick is taken. The rule says a player cannot be

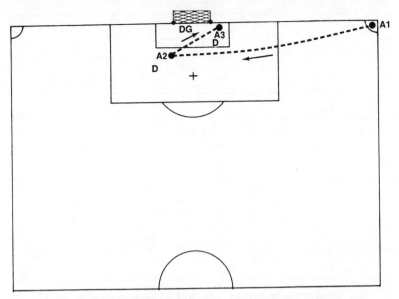

94. The corner-kick offside situation. Attacker A1 takes the corner kick. Attacker A3 does not have two players between himself and the goal. But at this instant he is not offside. The ball is received by attacker A2, who passes it directly to A3. A3 is now offside. Had A2 shot directly and scored a goal, the referee might have allowed the goal. On the other hand, he might have also disallowed it, ruling that A3 was interfering with play.

offside from this action. But if there are two attackers in what would be offside positions when the corner kick is taken and one of them gets to the ball and then passes to his colleague, the colleague is offside (see diagram 94). This applies to throw-ins, goal kicks, or when the ball is dropped by the referee.

The call is often a judgment one by the referee, but it is usual for the referee to be in the immediate area when these plays are made, in the best position to make the call.

The second judgment call covers interfering with play (diagram 95). The situation might be that play is way over on

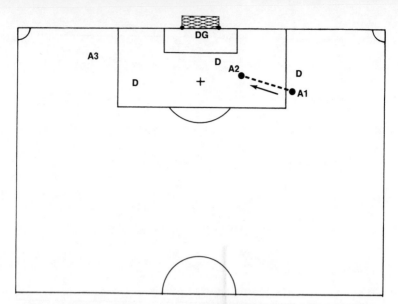

95. Interfering with play. Attacker A1 passes to attacker A2. On the far side of the field, attacker A3 is standing alone and nowhere near to the play. It could be argued that A3 is not offside, as he does not constitute an unfair advantage. But the call would almost certainly be offside because the goalkeeper could very well have his attention on A3. A3 thus is interfering with play.

the right-hand side of the field. An attacker has the ball. On the far left-hand side, an attacker is standing in what is obviously an offside position, but he is nowhere near the action of play nor is he involved in it.

Is he offside? Some referees would say no because the player is no threat and therefore is not contravening the rule from the viewpoint of obtaining an unfair advantage. On the other hand, it could be said that the goalie is focusing his attention on that player, thus taking his mind off the play action. This would be judged interference with play.

The offside rule was made to prevent an attacking team from taking an unfair advantage. The penalty for it is an indirect free kick awarded to the defending team.

FOULS

The severity of the foul committed dictates the type of free-kick penalty awarded. There are two categories of free kick: a direct kick or an indirect kick.

A direct kick means that the kicker may score directly without the ball having to touch or be played by anyone else. An indirect kick means that the ball has to be played or be touched by another player (from either team) other than the kicker before it crosses the goal line and a goal is scored.

The following are the intentional fouls for which a direct free kick is awarded:

Kicking or attempting to kick an opponent.

Tripping an opponent.

Jumping at an opponent.

Charging an opponent in a violent manner.

Hitting or attempting to hit an opponent.

Holding an opponent.

Pushing an opponent.

Handling the ball (except for the goalkeeper in his penalty area).

If any of these infringements are committed within the bounds of the penalty area, a penalty kick is awarded.

PENALTY KICK

The penalty kick is taken from the penalty spot. While the kick is being taken, all the players must be outside the penalty area. The goalkeeper, who should stand on the goal line between the goalposts, must not move his feet until the ball has been kicked into play. (The ball is in play once it has traveled its own circumference.)

If, after the referee has given the signal for the kick to be taken, the goalkeeper does move his feet, the referee will not stop the kick. But in that circumstance if a goal is not scored, then the kick must be retaken.

The following are the fouls for which an indirect free kick is awarded:

> Dangerous play (for example, high kicking).
> Charging albeit fairly but when the player charged is not playing the ball.
> Obstruction.
> Charging the goalkeeper.
> If the goalkeeper takes more than four steps while holding the ball.

In all cases the free kick is taken from the spot where the infringement occurred. All the opposing players must be at least 10 yards from the ball, unless the distance from the spot to the goal is less than 10 yards, in which case they may stand on the goal line.

CAUTIONS

A player may be cautioned if he persistently violates the rules of the game. The referee will hold up a yellow card in plain view for all to see. If that player continues to make infringements, the referee will then hold up a red card in plain view, and the player will be sent off the field. An example that would bring a yellow card would be arguing with the referee; a red card, using foul language.

THROW-IN

A throw-in is awarded when the whole of the ball crosses a touchline. The throw is awarded to the team that did not put the ball out of play.

The thrower must have both feet either on or behind the line when he makes the throw, the ball must be held in two hands, and the ball must come from behind and over his head.

The thrower may not touch the ball again until it has been played by another player.

If the throw-in is an improper one, then the throw is retaken by the opposing side. If the ball does not come into play from the throw—for instance, when the throw is made down the touchline but does not cross it into the field—the throw is retaken by the thrower.

GOAL KICK

A goal kick is awarded when the whole of the ball crosses the goal line—either on the ground or in the air—when it was last kicked by an attacking player.

The kick is taken from the goal area in that part nearest to the side of the goal where the ball went out of play. Opposing players must stand at least 10 yards from the ball until it has crossed the penalty-area line. The kicker may not touch the ball a second time until it is in play. If the ball does not cross the penalty line, the kick is retaken.

CORNER KICK

A corner kick is awarded when the whole of the ball crosses the goal line—either in the air or on the ground—when it was last kicked or touched by a defending player.

The kick is taken from the corner arc nearest to the side of the goal where the ball went out of play. A goal may be scored directly from a corner kick.

The kicker may not touch the ball a second time until it has been played by another player. Opposing players must stand at least 10 yards from the ball until it is in play.

The Referee

It has been said that refereeing a game of soccer is a thankless task. In fact, it rarely has to be. When it is, it is often because of poor control.

There is a growing trend in America to use two referees instead of one, plus two linesmen. This is particularly so in collegiate soccer. Linesmen are not authorized to control a game, only to assist the referee, whose decision on any matter is final. But the FIFA ruling is clear: one referee and two assistants—linesmen.

The laws state that a player shall be penalized if he intentionally commits an offense. The referee must decide immediately whether the act was intentional or accidental, and much of what a referee does is, therefore, based on his judgment.

A good referee very quickly gets a feel for the game and the players. He may, during the game, spot the odd elbow

96. Play on—advantage. The signal given when the referee sees an infringement but uses the advantage rule and indicates that play should continue.

97. Indirect free kick. The raised hand may also be open, face forward. The signal should be maintained until the kick is taken.

98. Direct free kick. The hand and arm clearly indicating the direction of the kick.

99. Penalty kick. The intention of the signal is obvious, and dramatic. The referee will be pointing to the penalty spot.

100. A goal-kick signal.

101. A corner kick. The referee indicating the corner flag.

102. A caution or expulsion, depending on the color of the card. Yellow for a caution, red for expulsion. In either case, the identity of the player concerned must be recorded. Most of the foul names are obvious descriptions of the infringement, that is, tripping, deliberate kicking, and so on.

dig here and there by a player and be influenced by such actions when that player is involved in a split judgment decision.

The responsibility for good conduct rests very firmly, in the first case, on the coach. It is his job to instruct his players how they should behave on the field. No talking back to the referee, no profanity, and, above all, no deliberate fouling.

Apart from trying to generate sportsmanship, there is a very good and practical reason for emphasizing the no-foul principle. Fouls bring penalties, either direct or indirect, and it is from penalties that goals are often scored by an opposing team.

Referees use standard signals on the field that are reinforced by the use of a whistle. Coaches and players should learn them in order to be able to take an advantage when it is offered. For example, it is not necessary to wait for the referee's whistle to take an indirect free kick provided the ball is placed in the proper position and is still before the kick is taken.

It is worthwhile training for a team to practice the various fouls so that the players are aware of what to avoid, and also what to expect. Invitational soccer competitions often give awards for good sportsmanship. They are highly valued awards worth working for.

International Styles of Play

Whether the styles of play adopted by various countries have anything to do with what might be called their national temperament or not is open to conjecture. Nevertheless, different countries have developed different styles.

The various styles are, traditionally, compared at the World Cup competition. Sometimes a national team will have adopted a slightly different style of play between two World Cup tournaments. For instance, England in 1966 played a 4–3–3 formation and won the cup, but when the team went to Mexico in 1970, they altered their formation to a 4–4–2. Their coach, Sir Alf Ramsay, had reasoned that Mexico's high altitude demanded accurate passing, instead of the traditional English fast game. (England lost in the quarterfinals to West Germany.)

Formations, of course, do not necessarily dictate a style of play, but they certainly contribute to it because it is the abilities of the players that produce the formation.

Three national teams demonstrate the most obvious variances in play: Brazil, West Germany, and England. Other nations show similarities to the predominant styles, as, for instance, the Dutch to the West German.

Brazilians are masters of nonchalant finesse and superb, individual ball control. They have supreme confidence, and their apparently effortless passing often appears casual. When they see a hole in the defense, they will strike with amazing speed. The Brazilian players are at their best when they can control the rhythm of the game. This is their great strength and their inherent weakness. Not particularly noted for their defense, if an opposing team can interrupt their dancelike rhythm, the Brazilians are thrown off balance and their confidence wanes.

The Brazilians have often been accused of faking injuries. It has been said they do this to break the concentration of their opponents. Trainers rush out onto the field; the game is held up. There have also been times when what seemed to be a minor trip was turned into a major foul by a Brazilian player hitting the dirt and grimacing in pain in order to persuade the referee to award a free kick.

The result has often been a goal because the Brazilians are the finest exponents of indirect and direct free-kick plays.

The West German style, which is admirably demonstrated on the "Soccer Made in Germany" television games, is completely different. The teams of the Bundesliga play a cerebral, controlled game. It is rare to see more than flashes of individual brilliance—their key is consistent, intelligent, superb soccer. There is a cool, instinctive logic about the way they play.

The West Germans never seem to tire themselves; their energy is conserved by using a series of calm passes—they are masters of the "keep-away" technique. Rarely drawn, they will retain possession of the ball and execute a pattern of bewildering moves that demonstrate more than anything that fixed-player position is a thing of the past.

One opposing coach came away from a World Cup final with statistics showing that the West Germans had successfully completed 83 percent of their passes—a fantastic achievement. That same coach also noted that the defense was often, surprisingly, caught napping.

The West German style of play is one of the easiest to analyze because of its pace—the slow buildup, then the marvelous instant (it seems) attack. Unfortunately, in a poor game it can tend to become boring, although in fairness few of the top games are ever that.

The English seem to enjoy their inconsistencies. Whereas the West German national team has had Helmut Schoen as their manager for years, in the same period of time the English have gone through Sir Alf Ramsay, Don Revie, and Ron Greenwood.

One's first impression while watching English teams play is their tremendous speed and hard tackling. In a poor game, though, it can look awful, almost as if the players don't have any idea of what they are supposed to be doing. But in a top game, when Liverpool is playing to form, for instance, there will be examples of soccer brilliance and courage.

The English player is expected to play all-out soccer for 90 minutes. Whereas the West Germans pace themselves, the English tear in, almost scrapping for the ball. Dribbling is a great factor in the English style of play, since stress is first placed on individual ability, which is then combined with the team concept.

On the international level you are never quite sure what to expect of the English. The West Germans and the Brazilians tend to be relatively predictable. The one thing you can be sure of with the English is drama, even if it turns out to rebound on them, but the spectator usually gets his money's worth.

What is the American style? So far, there isn't one. There are instances of individual style but not of a team, or as yet, national style, since many players on U.S. teams are not U.S. born.

The Future of Soccer in the United States

The only soccer style in the United States that can truly be called American is played by the youth teams, some college teams, and the handful of young men who make up the Olympic squads.

There is no successful U.S. professional soccer team that does not have more foreigners than nationals on the field of play. The one exception might be an American Soccer League team, which limits the number of foreigners on an eighteen-man roster to seven.

In Germany the bulk of the players are German; in Britain they are British; in Holland they are Dutch. In the United States they are from everywhere. This is so even in collegiate soccer; for example, the San Francisco Dons, who won the National Collegiate Championship four times, have used foreign players more often than nationals.

The NASL ruling is that if a team has a roster of seventeen players, six of them must be U.S. nationals. Beyond the seventeen-man roster, for every one foreign player signed, two U.S. players must be added.

But, that is the roster. On the field of play the rule only calls for a minimum of two U.S. nationals. For example, if we assume that the NASL has more than the minimum requirement of nationals on the field of play, say four, and that the ASL has five, of the total thirty-six teams and 396 players, 156 would be nationals and 240 foreigners. That means that of the total number of professional soccer players in the United States who might be actually playing and not sitting on the bench, only 39.3 percent would be Americans.

Of course, there are going to be variations; some teams may at one time or another play more nationals, others will play less. Nevertheless, it is probably not unreasonable to accept that when you watch a professional soccer game, you are watching a mixed bag of foreigners aided by a few Americans.

It should, however, be acknowledged that the foreign players—Pelé being the prime example—have generated tremendous interest in the sport. Without them it is doubtful if the game would have gained the popularity it is now enjoying in the United States.

Because of the franchise system, as opposed to the one in Europe where the game has been a national sport for years, U.S. soccer teams do not have clubs. That is, they do not have their own stadium or training facilities in which to operate. They have to rent the facilities, and these are generally U.S. football stadiums. Playing on fields designed for football has led to practical difficulties for U.S. soccer teams.

An NFL football field has fixed, universal dimensions: including the end zones, it is 120 yards long by 53½ yards wide. In soccer terms this is a very narrow field—only 3½ yards wider than the minimum requirement. This tends to produce a bunching of players in the middle, thus destroying almost entirely the open, wing style of play. Where possible, changes are being made, and some teams are now playing on wider fields.

The narrow field was the reason offered by the NASL

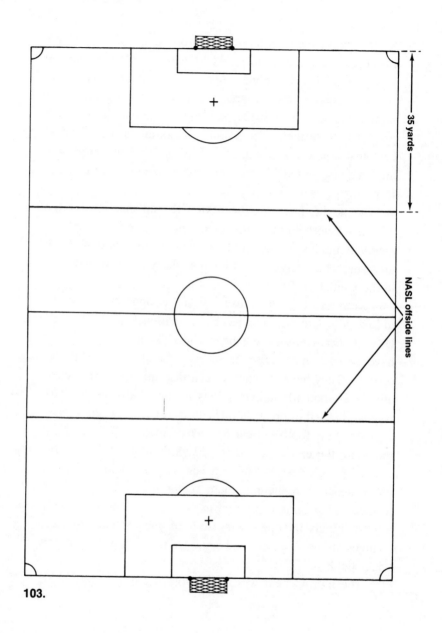

103.

for introducing, as an experiment, the 35-yard offside line.

Diagram 103 shows the new offside lines, which more or less correspond to the placing of a line across each defensive third. The purpose of the new line is to allow the forwards to be able to place themselves beyond the established halfway line before they become vulnerable to an offside call, thus "stretching" the game and alleviating the bunching caused by the narrow field.

There is a secondary motive for establishing the 35-yard offside line that appears to be far more attractive to the NASL. The original offside law was created to prevent forwards from obtaining an unfair advantage, and the new 35-yard line restores, to a certain extent, this advantage. Diagram 104 illustrates how a forward may gain greater penetration under the new rule, without fear of becoming offside until he is well into the opponents' half.

FIFA originally gave the NASL permission to use the new line on an experimental basis, but it seems FIFA now wants it removed, especially since American teams are the only ones in the world using it.

Youth-soccer teams do not use the 35-yard line, nor do collegiate players or the ASL. The NASL is not permitted to use it when playing international teams. The conclusion is that the line should go.

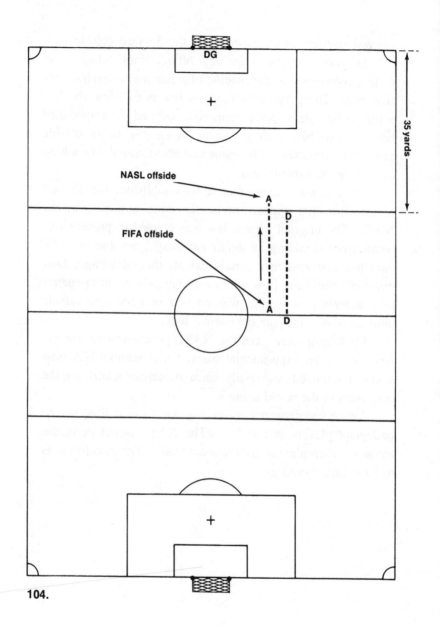

104.

A FINAL WORD—FOR PARENTS

A Philosophy

Soccer is a team sport. In youth soccer the game is played for the enjoyment and instruction of the players and for the development of good sportsmanship.

There are certain unwritten rules in youth soccer that everybody, whether playing or not, should remember. When the teams line up for the toss of a coin to decide who will choose to kick off or which goal to defend, it is proper for the team captains to shake hands.

If a player on the opposing team is injured but then continues to play, it is proper to show one's appreciation of his courage.

At the end of the game the losing side should gather together and cheer the winning. Similarly, the winners should reciprocate.

At the beginning of each season it is usual for coaches to call a meeting of the players he has selected, together with their parents, so that everyone may become acquainted and to give the coach an opportunity to express his attitude toward the game.

One attitude might be to tell parents and players that referees do not have an easy job, and it is inevitable that they will miss fouls and make mistakes. Those spectators who react to these mistakes by shouting at the ref from the side-lines might consider taking a referee course. Soccer needs good referees; what it does not need is adults making a poor example of themselves in front of young people.

Teams that have been playing together for a couple of years have, naturally, an established group and some idea of where their team might be going in the season. But with new teams, and particularly young ones, it might be worthwhile to explain to parents that while the purpose of the game is to win, winning is not the be-all and end-all of youth soccer.

Coaching—The New Season

Sooner or later many a spectator will want his involvement in soccer to go beyond just standing around on the side-lines yelling out encouragement. Many adults are frustrated teachers, and the idea of being able to mold a group of young players into a successful team is very attractive.

But whether you become a coach or not, it will add to the pleasure to be had from the game if you understand some of the problems—rather in the same way as knowing the rules helps one to understand the referee's viewpoint.

Probably the most difficult age groups to coach are the Under 14s and Under 16s. A team that has kept its players together as they mature has reason to believe that when they reach the older age groups some good soccer is going to be produced. And so it should. But, at around the same time, about half the team has entered puberty; a growth spurt is well under way and peer-group pressures will be very strong.

Meanwhile, the other half of the team, which has not reached puberty, will try to copy their more advanced colleagues.

The coach's attitude in these circumstances must, of course, be related to his personal relationship with his players. Nevertheless, there are some well-tried, albeit old-fashioned sounding, tactics that still seem to work rather well.

Planned physical exertion is an excellent way to reduce rebelliousness. Action appears to curb teenage resentments, and teenagers especially enjoy the glow the body produces after strenuous exercise, especially if it is directed toward a specific end product.

While a coach must be aware of the problems his players are going through, it may appear not unreasonable to seem to ignore them. There are other members of society— parents, teachers, and even the media—involved in trying to solve teenage problems, many of which disappear with maturity. The coach, as yet another adult authority figure, could prove valueless, and it could also ruin a potentially good soccer team.

A major problem in getting an Under-14 or Under-16 team into soccer shape will probably be trying to show the players that their kicking, passing, and the like are not quite as good as the players might think they are. A series of drills—one-on-one tackling, wall passing, and so on—can quickly prove boring and ineffective. The essential element here is to devise game situations in which the players will prove to themselves that they have shortcomings. This will tend to create within the player a motivation toward self-improvement.

Practices should start off with a lap or two around the track, players grouped in twin single file. It is essential that the coach impress on the players that regimentation of the formation be maintained. Players start off at a slow jog. On the whistle the last member of each of the two lines sprints forward to the front. The slow jog continues until the next whistle, when again the back pair sprint to the front. This should continue with the spaces between whistles becoming shorter. In fact, this exercise is a forerunner of what actually happens in a game: periods of slow movement with sudden action. More important, it is part of a training program where proper physical discipline is always maintained.

Following the opening drill, a routine start to every practice session, should come a simulated game. This particular practice game is designed to demonstrate to the players what they are doing wrong. If it is conducted properly, it won't be long before the players will either realize their errors or have them pointed out by their colleagues. (In other words, peer pressure can work for the coach.)

The players are divided into two teams. Generally, this will be about six or eight in each section. Often coaches like to play the defensive players against the attacking ones. Three-quarters of the field should be used.

There are a few rule changes for the practice game. First, no player is permitted to dribble, although he is allowed to move with the ball until challenged, at which time he must pass the ball. If a player does dribble, an automatic free kick is given to the other side.

No goal may be scored from a shot at goal (the game is played without goalkeepers); the ball must be walked across the goal line, or it may be headed in. Other than these, all the standard rules apply.

The coach, who should be on the field of play all through the practice session, will blow the whistle when he wants to stop the game. When the whistle blows, the team must freeze. At that point the coach instructs the players as to where they are going wrong and what to do about it.

The amazing thing about this drill is how well it works. Very few goals will be scored, and the players will, quite quickly at first, become fatigued. As the weeks go by, their stamina will increase. But the major factor is that when the game is stopped, everyone on the field will see which individuals are not doing what properly and why.

After a few sessions of this, the players will be very ready to accept advice—some will be giving it—about the personal shortcomings of each player. At the same time the passing expertise should improve dramatically, since it is the main thrust of the drill.

The team is now ready to accept further instruction, for they will have proved to *themselves* that they need it.

To be successful, coaching has to be positive. Having established in his mind the faults of his players, a coach must then concentrate on correcting them by example: showing a player how a certain skill can be improved.

It seems that short periods of maximum concentration followed by changes in activity work best. Periods of rest and discussion should also be interspersed with the drills. Very often a player will return to the next practice session much improved, even though he may not have been out on the field between practice sessions.

This isn't so surprising. As the body is controlled by the mind, it seems reasonable that the mind can practice on its own without always involving the body. Mental rehearsal of a skill seems to have great value, and a coach who has developed a good working relationship with his players is one who has encouraged this important aspect of training.

This is also the time when it might be wise to consider changing the positions of some players. The super-fast Under-12 winger of last season may have slowed up as he goes into his growth period. His greatest value may now be best exploited as a wing half. Similarly, a player may have grown much taller, and his added height could be put to good use in the center, either as the center forward or center half.

Each practice session should cover the introduction of a new and/or more advanced skill technique. This goes for the team as a whole as well as the individual players. It is essential that whichever new skill is taught, after the players have gone through practicing it, they demonstrate it on the field of play.

All skills should be practiced in as close to a game circumstance as possible. There will be some players who perform well off the field or in drills, but who do not perform as well in a game. Most soccer skills performed on their own are, of course, easier to do than when players are up against serious opponents.

The controlled scrimmage, much like the "freeze" passing game where the coach is on the field directing play, is vital if the players are to be molded into an effective team.

Coaching is more than just knowing the rules. It is a difficult and taxing job. Spectators and/or parents might keep this in mind if their home team, either youth or professional, does not appear to be doing too well.

In the end all the practice, soul searching, dedication, problems, and disappointments can produce a game of absolute bliss. It will be fun not only for the coach who has worried over his team and for the spectators who have watched them both win and lose, but most of all for the players.

105. This is the only moment of truth in soccer, when the ball lands up in the back of the net. This is what all the training, all the sweat, all the pain, is about. The finest game in the world.
Photo by Bob Thomas, Northampton, England